Ma and Pa.

A very Happy Christmas
with love from us all

John and Tania

Harry and Caroline.

THE COUNTRYSIDE
IN WINTER

OPPOSITE: *Golden eagle's eyrie, Scottish
Highlands*

THE COUNTRYSIDE IN WINTER

BRIAN JACKMAN

ILLUSTRATED BY BRUCE PEARSON

Hutchinson

London Melbourne Sydney Auckland Johannesburg

For Imogen

Century Hutchinson Ltd

17–21 Conway Street, London W1P 6JD

Hutchinson Publishing Group (Australia) Pty Ltd
PO Box 496, Hawthorn, Melbourne, Victoria 3122

Hutchinson Group (NZ) Ltd
PO Box 40-086, Glenfield 10, Auckland

Hutchinson Group (SA) Pty Ltd
PO Box 337, Bergvlei, 2012 South Africa

First published 1985

© Brian Jackman 1985
Illustrations © Bruce Pearson 1985

Set in Linotron Bembo by
Rowland Phototypesetting Ltd
Bury St Edmunds, Suffolk

Printed and bound in Italy by
Amilcare Pizzi s.p.a. Milan

British Library Cataloguing in Publication Data

Jackman, Brian
   The countryside in winter.
   1. Zoology – Great Britain   2. Winter –
   Great Britain
   I. Title
   591.54'3   QL255
ISBN 0 09 161810 X

CONTENTS

Partridge covey in snow

Acknowledgements

Many people helped me in the course of preparing this book. Some I knew already; others were strangers whom I now like to think of as friends. All gave willingly of their time and expertise, with great generosity, and the hours I spent with them are among my happiest winter memories.

First and foremost I would like to thank Bruce Pearson, whose evocative paintings and sketches grace these pages. Bruce is a first-class naturalist as well as a gifted artist who is happiest working in the field. In winter, this often required considerable powers of endurance: on more than one occasion he was forced to stop because the water had frozen on his brush! But the results have a life and freshness which could only have resulted from those long, cold, patient vigils out of doors.

I would also particularly like to thank Sir John Lister-Kaye, for true Highland hospitality, and for enabling me to realize my lifetime's ambition of seeing a wild British otter; Roger Lovegrove, of the Royal Society for the Protection of Birds, whose knowledge of the birds of Wales is matched only by his enthusiasm for being out in the field in all weathers; Rupert Brown and Martin Knowelden, generous hosts at Borley Mill and companions well versed in the ancient arts of pike fishing; Richard Treleaven, friend, painter, raconteur and guardian of the Cornish eyries, for many happy days sharing his obsession with the peregrine falcon; John Robinson, of the Nature Conservancy Council, who so kindly consented to act as my guide in Wyre Forest; Tony Holley, for entertaining me at his home on the Somerset Levels and giving me an insight into the fascinating world of the brown hare; Max Seaford, a former shipmate from National Service days, for joining me on a sea watch at Portland Bill when the summer migrants were leaving; and John Frankcom, of the Forestry Commission, for enabling me to observe the fallow deer rut in the New Forest.

Many other kind people provided both information and inspiration: Hugh Miles, Brian Rice, Everard Marsh, Dennis Bowman, Paul Henderson, Angela King and Sylvia, Lady Sayer. I should also like to mention Mike Shaw of Curtis Brown, my agent, a continual source of encouragement; Roger Houghton of Hutchinson for his unswerving confidence; my *Sunday Times* colleague Richard Girling, for his invaluable help with the text; and Norman Reynolds, who designed this book. Finally I should like to thank Sarah, my wife, without whose loyal support and companionship the book could not have been written.

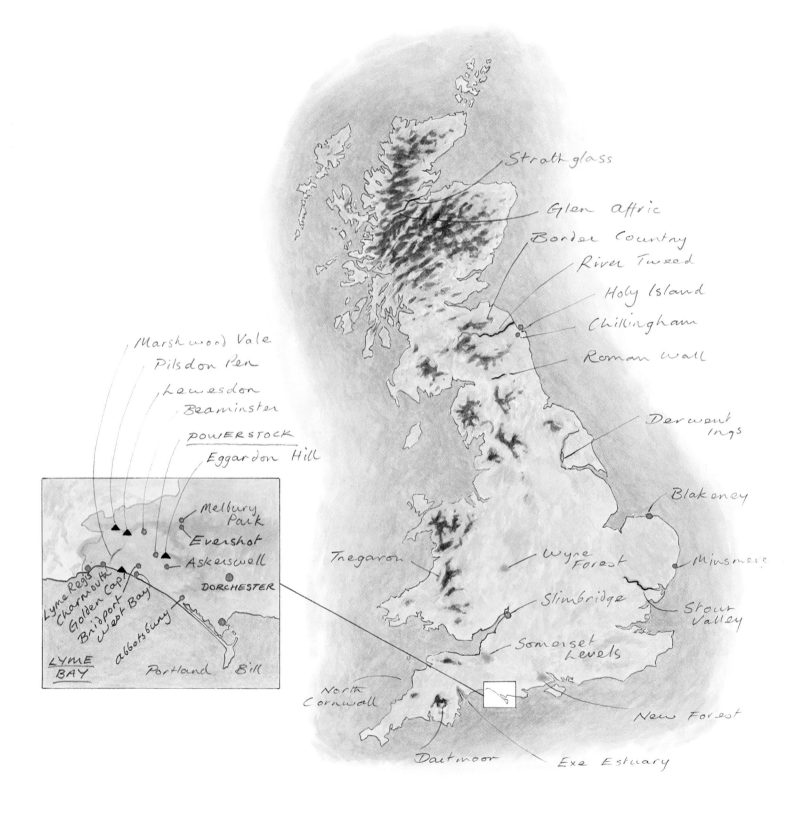

Strathglass

Glen Affric

Border Country

River Tweed

Holy Island

Chillingham

Roman Wall

Derwent Ings

Blakeney

Minsmere

Wyre Forest

Slimbridge

Stour Valley

Tregaron

Somerset Levels

New Forest

North Cornwall

Dartmoor

Exe Estuary

Marshwood Vale

Pilsdon Pen

Lewesdon

Beaminster

POWERSTOCK

Eggardon Hill

Melbury Park

Evershot

Askerswell

DORCHESTER

Lyme Regis

Charmouth

Golden Cap

Bridport

West Bay

Abbotsbury

LYME BAY

Portland Bill

INTRODUCTION

Winter in Britain is a marvellously quiet, introspective time. A feeling of gentle, brooding melancholy settles on the countryside. People are fewer. Horizons close in. Woods gather round. There is a sense of repose, a sinking down. The land sleeps. Yet it is never quite dormant, for winter is also a time of great migrations: the running of the salmon, and tumultuous movements of birds driven south to these shores by winters harsher than our own. It is a time to admire the extraordinary adaptability of wildlife, its resilience and tenacity.

It is a connoisseur's season, its colours muted, miraculous and austere. With the leaves fallen it is easier to appreciate the tracery of trees and the stark simplicity of bare horizons. The lanes are full of foxy smells. The fields are open to the sky, frosty and sublime. Somehow, in winter, among spectral woods where crabbed oaks are hunched against the wind, the past seems closer. You can feel it in your bones: the ancient spirit of the land, haunting and intangible. With it comes a sense of grandeur. You catch it on the lonely downs; in the East Anglian marshlands; on the cold Welsh hills; and nowhere better than in the Scottish Highlands when the corries echo to the autumn roaring of the stags, snow clouds begin to build up, and the unearthly music of migrating geese and Arctic swans falls across the dull glitter of the winter firths.

Most of all, though, winter is the English season, when the countryside becomes a watercolour wash of spinney and ploughland, forlorn mallard standing on frozen ponds and woodpigeon clattering into soft, hazy skies. That is why, every year when the days draw in, when mist floats over the fields at dawn and dusk and the smell of wood smoke hangs in the air, I feel a quickening of the blood, an anticipation of sights and sounds that keep me rooted in Britain when others may yearn for the warm south. So not for me the Mediterranean and its hot, singing colours. Deprived of frost and falling leaves and the sheer atavistic pleasure of toasting myself in front of an ash-log fire, I would feel such places to be no more than beautiful prisons.

My needs are simple. Just save me a few acres of sodden fields and streaming ditches, a scrap of stubble where pheasants can strut, and a buzzard mewing over Eggardon. That is why, of all places in the world, I choose to live in Dorset. No matter how long I stay here I shall not cease to love the village I call my home. I was not born to it, yet I count its quiet pleasures as the greatest of blessings. Familiarity does not loosen its hold on me. Rather, every walk is still a journey of discovery, enriched with incident: a dipper's nest, a fox surprised, a bullfinch in an apple tree; images of time and place to be stowed away and savoured long after, like good wine.

This book was conceived as a celebration of winter. It begins in October with the ripeness, colour and decay of autumn, when birds and mammals feast and fatten and all wildlife prepares for the lean months ahead. It ends in March, when the land emerges shriven and renewed to greet the returning spring. It is, in effect, an irregular diary, recording – with the aid of Bruce Pearson's beautiful paintings and sketches – observations of wildlife and countryside, both in my home parish and on a number of forays all over Britain to see some of the spectacular creatures – otter, peregrine, kite and eagle – which add so much drama to the land in winter. Most of the entries relate to a single winter, 1983–84, but I have fleshed them out with a few random notes from other years to provide a fuller picture.

So much of Britain is now a wasteland, wrecked and polluted beyond recall. So many fine landscapes have been trussed by power lines or sliced up by motorways into pockets of land too small to sustain a sense of distance and mystery. Ours is a countryside in tatters, its farmlands increasingly made more efficient at the expense of wildlife. Yet enough of the old, half-tame Britain still survives – in wood, marsh, moor and sea cliff – to support an extraordinary range of wild plants and creatures. If there is any purpose to this book other than a straightforward attempt to capture in words and pictures the magic of winter, then it is this: wild places and wild creatures still exist in many parts of Britain, and can be found if we are prepared to seek them out. Having found them, let us recognize and cherish them for what they are – the very fabric of our national heritage, priceless and irreplace-able.

Brian Jackman
Powerstock, Dorset
January 1985

9

OCTOBER

2 October
Portland Bill, Dorset

Autumn was here at last, and in its true colours, grey and overcast. For much of September, Dorset had basked in an Indian summer of golden days and mild nights. Even last week there had still been a few clouded yellow butterflies in the mushroom-smelling meadows, and a humming-bird hawk moth feeding on garden honeysuckle. But yesterday the weather broke. It rained all day – a relentless drizzle falling in fine curtains across the valley, completely obscuring the familiar contours of Eggardon, the great promontory hillfort whose grassy summit, framed by my kitchen doorway, commands the skyline east of Powerstock.

This morning the hill was still furred with mist, but the day held the promise of better things. In wet lanes awash with yellowing leaves I drove over Eggardon's Iron Age ramparts, then cut across country to the south, following the back roads towards Abbotsbury and the coast. On Abbotsbury Hill the cloud broke briefly, letting in shafts of silver light that fell across one of the finest views in England. In the foreground rose the medieval hilltop chapel of St Catherine. Behind it gleamed the brackish waters of the Fleet, held back from the sea by the immense curve of the Chesil Bank; and in the distance Portland Bill, a crocodile snout of solid limestone charging into the English Channel.

It had seemed to me that Portland was as good a place as any to begin a chronicle of winter. Together with those of Dungeness in Kent and Prawle Point in south Devon, its skies each spring and autumn are one of the great flight paths for millions of birds of passage. Here I could stand and feel the slow turn of the seasons, watching the last of summer drift away with the migrating swallows.

LEFT: *Portland Bill, Dorset*
OVERLEAF: *Eggardon Hill, Dorset*

The cuckoos are the first away, leaving Portland in mid-July. Last to go are the winter thrushes – redwings, fieldfares – and a straggle of blackcaps and goldcrests in November. But the mass of departing summer migrants builds up through September to peak in these first October days. Most birds cross the coast at night; redstarts, turtle doves, gangs of swifts, clouds of warblers, unseen rivers of whispering wings pouring out to sea under the stars.

Sometimes, however, if the weather closes in, the birds appear confused and settle in thick 'falls' upon the treeless fields of the Bill, where their arrival is eagerly awaited each year by birdwatchers from every part of Britain. For many years the Old Lower Lighthouse at the end of the Bill has been a bird observatory, where the migrants are caught in mist nets to be weighed, measured and ringed by ornithologists who are still trying to unravel the mysteries of bird migration.

Here, too, like moths to a lamp, come the 'twitchers' – birdwatching fanatics who will travel any distance for a glimpse of a rarity. This autumn a Pechora pipit had turned up – only the second sighting on the British mainland of a bird which breeds in Arctic Russia. And even as the twitchers were scouring Portland for a glimpse of it, another, still rarer, bird had dropped in – a Blyth's pipit, a species hitherto unknown in this country except as a skin in the Brighton Museum.

Portland Bill seemed exactly the right kind of place in which to encounter not only these unexpected vagrants but the twitchers themselves, stalking over the fields in Barbour jackets, bowed down under the weight of binoculars or shouldering telescopes with barrels like trench mortars. It's a weird bit of England – untidy, unloved, grievously misused: a grey stony fiefdom of castles, prisons, derelict quarries and radio masts, whose inhabitants are insular and superstitious (never say 'rabbit' to a Portland islander). At its northern end, below the Verne, lies the huge naval harbour: an English Gibraltar with nests of oil tanks, dockyards and warships, and 2000 acres of sheltered waters enclosed by jetties built with convict labour in the second half of the nineteenth century.

Below Southwell the open strip fields tilt seawards down a narrowing beak which ends at the sea-girt monolith of Pulpit Rock. The wooden shacks that litter this southern tip of the island are boarded up for winter. The soil is thin – the stone pokes through. There is always a wind, and even on a calm day it carries the sound of the Portland Race, the fierce rip tide which streams south from the Bill in a turmoil of churning water. Yet for all its slovenliness this barren promontory has a strange fascination which cannot be denied. It is a natural pier, a vantage point from which to observe the sea not from the landsman's shallow shores but from a deep-water platform where the Race seethes and grumbles and the westering coast is a receding shadow beyond the immense bight of Lyme Bay.

With a birdwatching friend of mine, a regular visitor to Portland, I settled down for a sea watch, out of the wind with my back to a ledge beneath the obelisk which stands near Pulpit Rock. The horizon was hazy. To the east, so faint was the Purbeck coast that I could barely make out the pale scar of Lulworth Cove. Offshore, due south of the Bill, a half-dozen fishing boats, hunting the autumn runs of bass, bucked at the western approaches to the Race. Sometimes they disappeared completely between the steeply charging waves. Further out to sea, the white water breaking over the Shambles Bank looked like the breaching of giant whales. It was here, on 5 February 1805, that the *Earl of Abergavenny*, an East Indiaman of 1200 tons, outward bound from Portsmouth for Bengal and Canton, struck the shoals and slid away to sink in twelve fathoms, drowning 233 men and one woman in Dorset's worst-ever shipwreck.

In autumn there is always a steady passage of seabirds moving down the Channel. They come from Scotland and the Baltic: seaduck, skuas, auks and terns, and large numbers of waders. But it needs a good onshore wind to bring them close to the Bill. Today they were few: a couple of common terns; two guillemots flickering fast and low in the troughs; a solitary gannet, dazzling white, soaring to the west; and a pack of scoters – coal-black seaduck – bound for the Bay of Biscay where they would pass the winter.

Gannet

Inland was a different story. From a wooden hide in the observatory gardens I watched spotted flycatchers, redstarts and a lone turtle dove. In the bushes nearby was a pied flycatcher – a new species for me – a bird of the Welsh oak valleys, looking oddly out of place on this treeless coast.

My companion and I walked out into fields alive with meadow pipits. Wheatears bobbed white rumps on anthills and fence posts. In bramble thickets scorched brown by mid-September gales chiffchaffs and goldcrests were moving like mice, hunting insects under the leaves. We came to a deserted building on whose roof a black redstart had been spotted that morning, but did not find it. Instead, as we retraced our steps, a sparrowhawk appeared, flinging up clouds of birds in its wake. Some followed, mobbing the hawk, but it seemed hardly to notice as it turned away in a long, glancing dive over the hill and out of sight behind Eight Kings Quarry. Even after the hawk had gone, its presence seemed to hang in the air; the sky was full of linnets, pipits and starlings, all rising and falling in the fading light. When morning came, many of the migrant flocks would be gone and it would be six months before Dorset would see them again.

10 October

Powerstock, Dorset

I have spent the past twenty winters in a cottage which my wife and I found by chance in 1965 – a tumbledown hulk no bigger than a haystack, perched on the lip of a narrow valley. It had stood derelict for so long that part of the thatch had caved in. Inside, the walls were stained with damp. The stairs were riddled with rot, and when I tried to climb them they broke beneath my feet and I fell into a cupboard festooned with fungi. The ceilings were low, and the place was altogether much too small – two up, two down, with a Victorian lean-to kitchen. But the stone walls were sound, the views were magnificent and it caught the sun from dawn to dusk. It cost £800 to buy and another £2000 to make habitable, and it took every penny we had. Ten years later we demolished the old lean-to and built a bigger kitchen, installed a Rayburn and added an upstairs studio. Today the house is still too small but I cannot imagine living anywhere else.

Framed in the window as I write, Dorset spills southward, a rumple of slopes, woods and hills. That way lies the sea, only four miles distant. Outside the house is a green lane. Beyond it the meadows plunge to a hidden stream where small trout hover under mossy alders. On the other side of the combe, among the last of the cider apple trees, sheep are grazing. There is a thatched stone cottage, a bridge, a footpath through the fields.

We live in a backwater on the way to nowhere, buried among hills too steep to plough. Chameleon country, always changing, serene in summer, withdrawn in winter, perhaps haunted, though never hostile. Downstream the hills rise and tumble into Devon, blue with distance, defining the edge of the Marshwood Vale. Upstream, gnarled hedge-row oaks claw their way to the foot of the downs, to the flanks of Eggardon, the last frontier of the southern chalk, where the West Country begins. I have loved landscape for as long as I can remember, and this sleepy hollow in the midmost heart of the magic triangle bounded by Dorchester, Beaminster and Lyme Regis is the very quintessence of the English countryside.

West Dorset has the look and feel of a separate county. It is its own place, a land apart, with its own clearly defined frontiers. It lies hard up against the borders of Devon and Somerset, with the sea at its back and the high chalk to the east. Here is England at its best, a balanced compromise between man and nature. Slow to change, well farmed on the whole, but with an abundance of rough corners, old pasture and boggy bottoms in which wildlife still thrives. The hedgerows, not yet grubbed out to make arable prairies, still harbour primrose clumps and whitethroats' nests. There never was much elm, so West Dorset was

Fieldfares and redwings feeding on hawthorn berries

spared the devastation of Dutch elm disease which laid bare the landscapes of south Somerset. Here the trees are oak, ash and hazel, and the woods are thick with roe and fallow deer. I know where wild snowdrops grow, and bee orchids. There are badgers at the bottom of my garden. In Dorset you can still find, for the time being at least, echoes of an older England which elsewhere have long since fallen silent.

Powerstock is a small village, pretty without being self-conscious, with stone houses and a few thatched cottages straggling up the hillside. At its centre, where five lanes meet, stands the church of St Mary, a gilded weathercock turning in the wind on its yellow stone tower. The churchyard is a place of deep and ancient silence; a wild garden of dark yews and leaning headstones, weeping ash and springtime snowdrops – although when we first moved to the village it was also the home of Lazarus, the one-eyed church cat, a black-as-midnight feral tom who lived in a sepulchre and made sleep impossible with his amorous serenading.

The Normans built the church and its crooked chancel arch in the twelfth century. On the hilltop just outside the village they also built the motte and bailey earthwork, known as Humpy Castle. Tradition says that the site is older; that the Saxon king, Athelstan, had his winter palace on this spot; and that later, when King John visited Powerstock to hunt deer, he kept a mistress here. But today nothing remains except mounds and ditches.

One of the pleasures of living here is that the countryside begins quite literally at the doorstep; there is no need to drive to find somewhere to walk. Through the gate, down the lane to the stream, and suddenly one is in deep countryside, walled about by hazel hedgerows and steep grassy slopes. This morning, as usual, a trout hung in the pool below the footbridge and shot upstream as soon as it saw me. There were still a few mushrooms in the field beyond – enough to fill a bag for tomorrow's breakfast. Higher up the valley, towards Castle Mill Farm, cider apples glowed like lanterns in the derelict orchard. Wrens scolded from brittle stems of head-high hogweed, and blackbirds pecked at windfalls in the long grass.

I have never learned to love rough cider; but if you live in the West of England there is no doubt that it is the *vin du pays*. In the counties of Somerset, Devon and Hereford, where the real *grand cru* stuff comes from, cider orchards are as common as church towers, and there are still a few traditionalists making farmhouse cider on a commercial scale, sandwiching the apples between layers of straw and squeezing them in wooden presses.

Shorn of its tipsy hayseed image, cider has become acceptable, even fashionable as a party drink, a take-home habit, something to use instead of wine in the kitchen. Of course nowadays most of it is not the rough draught stew of yesteryear, but a sparkling, carbonated, keg beer equivalent, mass-produced and bottled in factories. So popular has it become that demand threatens to outstrip supply, and tanker-loads of apple juice have to be shipped over from Normandy to make up the shortfall. But the French orchards, like our own, are going fast and are not being renewed.

As a result, some cider firms have been encouraging local growers by offering them maiden trees at cost, planted and looked after free of charge for the first few years. Such an orchard exists just over the hill at Melplash, and very prolific it looks too, with its compact and heavy-cropping bush varieties all producing the classic bitter-sweet apples which give West Country cider its special flavour. But the traditional orchards, with their standard trees widely spaced at no more than forty to the acre, are sadly no longer economic. Relics of a bygone age when cider flowed freely in the harvest fields, most are long past their prime and following the heavy horse into oblivion. Not for much longer shall we see the wasteful old standards with their splendidly bacchanalian names: Hangydown, Brown Snout, Slack-ma-Girdle. The oldest trees have stood here since the reign of Edward VII, hoary with lichen, infested with mistletoe, their hollow trunks occupied by generations of starlings and woodpeckers. Every spring these septuagenarian greybeards still make the valleys glorious with their pink and white blossom. But in late September the apples are left to rot where they fall. And every winter, when the gales come, more trees are blown down and are not replaced.

At the head of the combe beyond Castle Mill Farm stands a squat oak overgrown with ivy, in whose dark shadows an odd, pale shape caught my eye. As I stared, it materialized into a barn owl and sailed silently out across the fields. Not far away I found another of its roosting places, and pellets of fur under a railway arch splashed with white droppings.

In less than ten years the disused railway track that runs up against the combe has been almost overwhelmed by rampant weeds and scrub. Toadflax and wild strawberries have rooted themselves in the ballast, together with rosebay willowherb and marching spires of mullein. In summer this was a favourite place for basking adders. Now the banks on either side were laden with fruit: a brilliant wild harvest of rose hips and guelder rose, clusters of bryony, spindle and dogwood, dusky sloes the colour of grapes, and hawthorns dripping scarlet berries. The sun shone briefly, and a red admiral butterfly sat with open wings, sucking juice from a blackberry with a tongue like a watchspring.

Every morning the fields were seeded with dew. As yet there had been no frost, but already the leaves of the field maples had lit yellow fires in the hedgerows. The woods were damp and full of fungi. The smell of decay was in the air, rank and stale. There was a sense of sadness and repose, as poignant as wood smoke. The old year was dying.

11 October
Melbury Park, Dorset

Stone lions guard the gateway to Melbury House, home of the Lady Teresa Agnew. The house, built in the sixteenth and seventeenth centuries, is not open to the public, but a right of way crosses the park from Evershot to Melbury Osmond – a distance of less than two miles. It is easy walking and in autumn, when the wooded hillsides and chestnut avenues are changing colour, Melbury becomes everyone's dream of an English deer park.

There were deer everywhere under the trees. Most were fallow deer, browsing or resting in peaceful herds; but I also saw a number of red deer, including several fine stags. One, a huge five-pointer with a leonine mane and clods of grass hanging from his tines, belched and grunted in the throes of the rut, but no rival took up the challenge.

The day was windy, with low cloud bringing an occasional spatter of rain from the southwest. The wind passed over the beechwoods with a sound like crashing surf, whipping away the first dying leaves. So far it had been a mild autumn. No frosts yet; but soon all the broad-leaved trees would shed their leaves, then being better able to withstand winter. Already the horse chestnuts, invariably among the first to turn colour, were yellowing, and the grass beneath them was littered with fallen conkers. I searched among the burst shucks and gathered a handful. They smelled sour and floury, reminding me of my childhood. Their glossy skins, whorled and polished dark as rosewood, are still my earliest memory of autumn.

Melbury is Dorset's blue-grass country, where thoroughbred horses prance in paddocks behind stout oak railings. Swallows were still swooping over the grass, and it was strange to think that five weeks later they could be hawking for insects in the sunlight of the African veldt.

Red admiral butterfly

In Melbury Osmond the road dips down through a watersplash with a pavement high above. There are grey stone houses under grey-green thatch, iron railings painted white, and a farm like a dream of childhood: thatched stone barn, free-range hens, a gaggle of geese beside a stream, and a dun horse that came to the gate to nuzzle my hands. Thomas Hardy knew this village well. His mother was a poor village girl, who married in the church of St Osmond on 22 December 1839. The present building dates mostly from the eighteenth century, but the curious carved stone set in the north wall of the sanctuary is a relic from the original Saxon church. Some people believe that it represents the sheep found in a bush by Abraham; but the stone is so deeply eroded that it might just as easily be one of the writhing, stylized dragons of Anglo-Saxon mythology.

Outside, Michaelmas daisies bloomed in cottage gardens. Holly berries were ripening early; and a solitary sunflower, its drooping head the size of a dinner plate, stood against a south-facing wall like a valediction for the vanished summer.

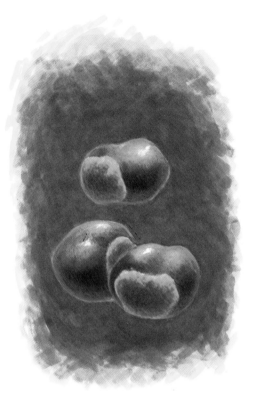

16 October
Charmouth, Dorset

All night long it had blown a gale, the wind ranting so fiercely that it had driven the rain beneath the kitchen door and made puddles on the floor. But by mid-morning the eye of the storm had passed and the cloud began to break, revealing bright gleams of sun between the squalls.

Horse chestnuts

At Charmouth the tide was up. An angry sea, churned to the colour of *café au lait*, hurled itself at the coast in long white rollers that broke with thundering force. The shock of their fall filled the air with a fine salt spray that hung like a haze under the cliffs, and the gasp of pebbles sucked back in the undertow was loud enough to drown all speech. In places the wind and rain and buffeting seas had brought fresh falls of mud and stone slithering down the cliffs to spill in dark aprons of ooze across the shingle; even as I watched, another ledge gave way with a sudden roar of spinning rock and crashed on the beach hundreds of feet below.

On either side of Charmouth the coast is inherently unstable. The crumbling cliffs are forever cracking and foundering in gigantic landslips of soft clays and brittle shales; and it is then, after a fresh fall has been washed clean by winter storms, that the fossil hunters gather.

Between Lyme Regis and the flat, 600-foot summit of Golden Cap, a mile east of Charmouth, fossils are as plentiful as currants in a Christmas pudding. Here in unrivalled abundance can be found the remains of the strange and beautiful creatures which lived when Dorset's Blue Lias bedrock was being laid down: coiled ammonites the size of French horns; bullet-shaped belemnites once known as 'devil's thunderbolts', but in reality only the backbones of primitive cuttlefish; and nautiloids which can be sawn in half and polished until the calcite cavities of their shelly inner chambers shine like petrified honey. There are sea lilies, too: fragile fans turned to stone and then delicately gilded by iron pyrites. That same fool's gold also glitters on countless small ammonities scattered in the sand like dull coins.

Some of the best specimens are hidden in nodules of dove grey limestone, and it takes a keen eye to spot one. To the uninitiated such a fossil looks like just another pebble on the beach: a wave-worn rock the size of a dinner plate. But the true fossil hunter will recognize it immediately. Turning it on edge, he taps it smartly with hammer and chisel until the rock splits neatly open, like the twin halves of an almond shell, revealing the perfectly preserved ram's-horn spiral of a fossil ammonite that last saw the light of day more than 150 million years ago.

All the cliffs here are full of such treasures; every seam is stuffed with them. The whole coast is a giant, multi-layered sandwich beginning with dark and sinister Black Ven marls, going on to shales-with-beef, belemnite marls and greensand ammonite beds topped with a tawny spectrum of more youthful loams and sandstones. But the bargain basement, the foundation stone underpinning this entire fantastic cross-cut through prehistoric time, is the famous Dorset Blue Lias, graveyard of the great marine reptiles of the early Jurassic world. These blue-grey slabs of banded limestone are the oldest rocks in Dorset, and when you walk upon them, as you can at low tide on the beach below the cliffs of Black Ven, you are stepping on a prehistoric floor laid down by the sediment of the vanished seas in which most of England lay immersed 180 million years ago. Then the warm Jurassic waters swarmed with life. Ammonites and belemnites crawled and swam in their millions among the sea lily meadows. Barrel-bodied plesiosaurs reared their long necks above the waves. Fierce ichthyosaurs – the giant ocean-going fish-lizards whose remains were first discovered at Lyme Regis by the young Mary Anning in 1810 – surged through the shallow seas in search of prey. The monstrous megalosaurus roamed the marshy deltas, while nightmarish pterosaurs, airborne reptiles with tooth-armoured beaks, sailed overhead.

Fossil ammonites

When they died the creatures sank to the bottom, there to vanish beneath the fine and ceaseless drizzle of blue-grey sediment. And there they remain, buried and compressed under the weight of the millennia – teeth, scales, shells, bones, the charnel house of an entire epoch preserved and hidden until one day a storm blows, a chunk of cliff falls away, and a sharp chisel splits open a limestone nodule to let in the sunlight of the twentieth century.

20 October
New Forest, Hampshire

A full moon still hung in the awakening sky when I called at the cottage on the outskirts of Lyndhurst, but John Frankcom was already up and about. Like all New Forest keepers, he is used to getting up early. Together we walked out into the windless dawn, to the high seat in the Forest at Parkhill Inclosure. There, with luck, I might see the fallow deer in rut.

Many an ancestral English park has its herd of dappled fallow deer. They are a sight familiar even to Londoners, who can see them in Richmond and Bushey Parks. But there are some truly wild herds, too, as well as those which have escaped in almost every English county; and there have been fallow deer in the New Forest for longer than anyone can remember – perhaps since Roman times.

Not all fallow deer have the dappled chestnut coats of the ornamental parkland herds: in colour they range from donkey brown to almost black, and white animals are not uncommon. They also differ from the ornamental animals in size. Here there are no fat fields to feed in; they must forage in the forest, and are therefore altogether leaner and lighter, although the bucks still produce good heads.

The fawns are born in May and it takes a full year for their first antlers to appear: twin stubby spikes sheathed in velvet until August. In its second summer the young male with its six-inch antlers is called a pricket. The second head is shed in April or May, and a fortnight later a new growth develops, with brow and trey tines and broad-bladed ends spreading fingerlike tips known as spellers. At the age of seven the head will be at its most magnificent, after which the antlers will regress and never be so fine again.

The bucks spend the summer as solitary wanderers, or sometimes join together in small bachelor groups. In August, when their new antlers are fully grown, they are eager to rid themselves of the madly itching velvet. On hot summer days, when it becomes unendurably irritating, they rub their antlers against trees and bushes until hard bone shows clean beneath and every last bloodstained scrap of velvet is peeled away.

The dawn still held a hint of frost when we set out, and although the forest oaks were still green the birch and bracken had turned to gold and the beechwoods flared with October colour. We walked down the rushy rides in silence. This part of the forest was new to me; but for John Frankcom it was familiar territory, a regular part of his beat, bordered by Lyndhurst, Brockenhurst and the Beaulieu River. Thirty-two years a keeper, he has spent the last twenty-four in the New Forest, and his sharp eyes are quick to spot the fleeting shapes of deer, fox and sparrowhawk. 'Keepers are not made,' he says. 'They are born.'

Fallow deer in rut, New Forest, Hampshire

He pointed to a disturbance in the leaf mould where badgers had been grubbing for worms and beetles during the night. Farther on we came to a black wallow where a buck had rolled and trampled to mark his territory and had thrashed his antlers in a wreckage of hazel. Normally the rut begins during the second week of October and lasts until early November. This year, perhaps because of the dry summer, it was only just beginning. But now the veteran bucks, seven- or eight-year-olds in their prime, would rend the air with groans of love. The deer once had regular rutting grounds which they used year after year; but nowadays there is too much disturbance, says Frankcom, and the bucks have been forced to move away. When a master buck does manage to establish himself with maybe half a dozen does, he marks out his territory, as we had just seen, thrashing bushes with his antlers until the branches are stripped and shining. Furiously he paws at the black humus beneath. Clods of moss fly from his hoofs until he has dug and trampled a muddy pit impregnated with the smell of his urine. This is his stamping ground, and here he will stay, keeping a jealous eye on his harem as the ever-watchful younger bucks wait for a chance to sneak in.

Poaching has always been a problem in the New Forest. Venison fetches a good price in Southampton, with no questions asked if you know the right contacts. In the old days it was men with guns. Now the poachers are more cunning. They go 'lamping' with lurchers, or even crossbows. Only two days earlier a New Forest pony had bled to death at this spot, a crossbow bolt lodged in its throat.

The wet earth underfoot was deeply imprinted with deer slots, but there was no sound except for an early robin, and the dark voice of a carrion crow deeper in the woods. Everywhere dead branches lay where they had fallen under the stag-headed oaks, to be consumed by mould and fungi. The leaves, too, had begun to fall, covering the mosses with a brittle carpet.

We came at last to the high seat, a skeletal watchtower of planks and poles supporting a rough platform 15 feet above the ground. There we would be unseen if the deer approached. We sat and waited. Our breath condensed in small clouds, drifting upwards, but no deer came. At eight o'clock a pale wash of sunlight touched the tops of the oaks. Slowly, over the next hour, we watched it slide down the mossy boles until it lit the dry leaves beneath. The air was so still that I could hear the winnowing wings of woodpigeons passing overhead. Then, for the first time, I heard another sound: the rhythmic, rasping grunt, like a distant motorbike being kick-started, of a fallow buck in rut. Again the buck threw down his challenge: a weird, primeval sound, an echo of the Saxon wildwood. This time he was answered, and soon there came a furious clashing of the rivals' antlers.

The forest fell quiet again. In front of the high seat stood an old beech stump, lipped with fungus. A treecreeper was working its way up the shattered trunk; it moved in a series of spasmodic jerks, swift as a mouse, supporting itself by pressing its tail against the bark as it paused to probe for spiders.

By ten o'clock the sun was slanting strongly through the trees, throwing sharp shadows across the close-nibbled lawns and dying bracken. Against the light the beeches glowed more gloriously than ever. Suddenly a fallow buck announced his presence with a grunt and stepped into the clearing from the dense understorey of holly. It was an impressive entrance: the wide, upcurving antlers held proudly erect, the sharp brow tines trailing moss, the thick coat stained and blackened where he had rolled and wallowed. Now he came towards the high seat. In the silence I could hear the faint tread of his hooves on the dry leaves as he stepped over a fallen branch. He did not see us, even when he passed almost directly beneath the seat, but as he cut our scent he started in alarm and trotted away towards Spaniard's Hole.

By 11.30 the forest was filling with Saturday strollers. The deer would lie low until evening, so we abandoned our hide and walked back to Lyndhurst. There I said goodbye to John Frankcom and drove towards Beaulieu. On the heathery commonlands at Beaulieu Road Station, horsemen with hunting whips were rounding up the forest cattle and driving them into a stockade by the railway line.

At Buckler's Hard, the Beaulieu River slid quietly seawards between tawny saltings to the mad xylophone jangle of wire yacht rigging slapping against masts. It was strange to think that these blue waters have their beginnings in the forest only a mile or two from the deer's rutting ground. There, it is little more than a gravel ditch filled with leaves. Here, it is a tidal river, smelling of the sea.

Nearby, at the Master Builder's House Hotel and Restaurant, oak logs were burning in an open fire, and there was venison for lunch. Here in the late eighteenth century lived the master shipwright Henry Adams, who built the wooden ships of Nelson's navy out of New Forest oak. In all, twenty-nine of his ships were launched from the stocks at Buckler's Hard, including the *Agamemnon* (sixty-four guns), *Swiftsure* (seventy-four guns) and *Euryalus* (thirty-six guns), of Trafalgar fame. An oak must grow for a hundred years before it can be felled for shipbuilding, and the demands of the Navy were more than the New Forest alone could fulfil; yet local trees provided much of the valuable 'compass' timber – the stout posts and curved ribs which

OPPOSITE: *Fallow deer sketched during the rut*

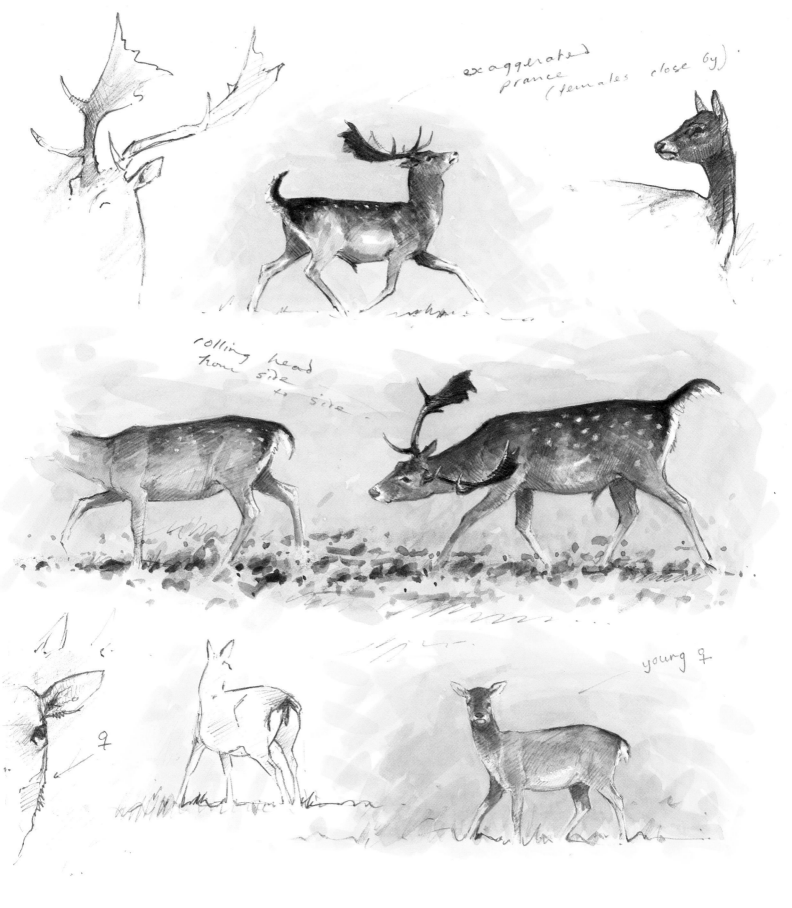

exaggerated prance (females close by)

rolling head from side to side

young ♀

♀

could be shaped with minimum effort from the oak's crooked branches. It took two thousand mature trees to build the *Agamemnon* in 1781; and by 1805 – the year of Trafalgar – there were perhaps one and a half million oaks afloat in the service of the Royal Navy.

At six o'clock I returned to the high seat for the final hour of daylight. Tomorrow it would be dark an hour earlier, for this was the last day of British summertime. The wind had died, and dusk was coming down with a certainty of frost. In the stillness I could hear the needle-thin cries of goldcrests and long-tailed tits hunting for insects in the leaves above. Somewhere a magpie chuckled. A wren ticked crossly as a pony ambled across the clearing. Light faded on oaks, glades, lawns and rides. The sun was down, but the western sky still gave out an orange glow between black trunks as the forest filled with shadow. The picnicking families and weekend walkers had gone long ago. The forest was sunk in a dungeon of silence, and I was alone. Far away in the direction of Thorn Hill a tawny owl hooted; and then, unmistakable in the frost-prickling air, a buck began to grunt again.

29 October
Hadrian's Wall, Northumberland

A hard time they must have had, those Roman garrisons of long ago, patrolling Hadrian's Wall. At Crag Lough Wood the wind shook the pines as if it were trying to hurl them into the lough below, where white horses charged the reedy shores in a welter of driven spray.

For anyone in search of fresh air and open space, Northumberland has plenty of both to spare; and there are few better ways to cleanse the dust from city lungs than to walk on the wall in an autumn gale. Striking west from Vercovicium, the Roman fort at Housesteads, it was easy to see why those canny soldiers chose this place to build their wall from coast to coast across the throat of Britain. Here the north-ward-rolling hills fall sheer in a frozen wave of dour grey dolerite known as the Whin Sill – with the long, thin line of the wall itself snaking over the crests; east over the Knag Burn and King's Hill to Carrawburgh; west by way of Cuddy's Crags to Steel Rigg and the Nine Nicks of Thirlwall.

I had spent the morning wandering around Vindolanda, a Roman fort just south of the wall on the Stanegate frontier. Here the *vicus*, or civilian settlement, has been excavated, and the museum is full of poignant relics. There are piggy banks kept by Roman children, and

Fieldfare on hawthorn

letters from home in the form of tablets: 'I have sent you two pairs of sandals. . . .' And you can see a reconstructed Roman kitchen with a bracken-strewn floor and wild duck hanging from the rafters.

But the greatest relic is the wall itself, seen at its most dramatic in the rugged stretch between Housesteads and Bogle Hole. The wind blew from the west and I walked in the teeth of it, following the wall as it rose and fell on its roller-coaster way to the Solway shore. The air was full of flying leaves, stripped from the sycamores that swayed with the hissing pines in walled spinneys. Through binoculars I could see a huddle of whooper swans sheltering at the western end of Greenlee Lough; but otherwise the world seemed devoid of birds. To the south, beyond General Wade's old military road, built after the suppression of the 1715 Jacobite Rebellion, bleak shafts of sunlight raked the South Tyne Valley between each furious squall. To the north, only the dark and distant cohorts of Forestry Commission pinewoods have altered a landscape of bracken, bent-grass and rushy turf which would still be recognizable to the men who manned the wall 1700 years ago.

'Hadrian was the first to build a wall, eighty miles long, to separate the Romans from the Barbarians.' This single sentence is the only reference in ancient literature to the formidable barricade which marked the turbulent northwest frontier of the Roman Empire for 250 years. The wall was begun in AD 122. By the time it was finished more than a million cubic yards of stone had been built into it, not only in the 10 foot thick walls but also in the string of forts, turrets and milecastles which stretched from Wallsend on the Tyne to Bowness on the Solway, holding thirteen thousand men when the garrisons were at full strength.

Its builders could not have guessed that their wall would still be standing long after the Roman Empire itself had been overrun. When the last troops departed, in AD 400, the fortifications were left to rot. The wall was cannibalized by generations of farmers who used it as a ready-made source of building stone, and whole lengths were carted away by General Wade to lay the foundations of his military road. Yet what remains is still the biggest single landmark ever laid across the face of Ancient Britain. In its own stark way the Roman wall is a far more powerful memorial than any classical temple or tessellated pavement; it forms an enduring monument to the boldness and vision of the invading legions, and to the stoicism of the local tribes – the Brigantes and the Votadini – who lived for four hundred years in the shadow of Rome but whose spirit was ultimately unquenchable.

Between Greenhead and Chesters the wall lies within the North- OVERLEAF: *Hadrian's Wall, Northumberland*

umberland National Park, with the Pennine Way following it as far east as Rapishaw Gap, where the path swings away towards Bellingham and the Cheviots. It is grand walking country, but of all the walkers it has attracted over the years few can have matched William Hutton for age, endurance or eccentricity. Hutton was seventy-eight when he walked the wall in 1801, having already trudged from Birmingham to Lakeland. Not for him the sturdy boots and sensible anorak of the modern fell walker. He completed the entire journey in the same black suit and single pair of shoes, and carried an umbrella in case it rained. His only concession to comfort was to undo the buttons of his waistcoat when the weather was too hot. In this manner, rising at four every morning, he walked the wall from end to end in both directions – and then walked all the way back to Birmingham.

But today the fells were deserted. The only signs of life were the sheep which came spilling out of a smout, or sheep creep, which had been built in the wall for the flocks to pass through. They were, appropriately I thought, Roman-nosed mules: a hybrid cross between the hardy Scottish Black-face ewe and a Border Leicester tup.

Beyond Highshield Crags the wall was stepped by its Roman builders to keep its courses horizontal as they descended a steep, grassy slope. In the next gap is a well-preserved milecastle site, and beyond that the path dives down the deep cleft in the Whin Sill at Cat Stairs. Then up again over Peel Crags, past Peel Cottage, where a fortified Border pele once stood, and on by way of Whinshields Crags, 1260 feet above sea level, with views of Criffell beyond the Solway on clear days, to Shield on the Wall, with the wind buffeting and the clouds racing, and on over Cawfield Crags, past inbye and outbye, among wide green fells where curlews call and you wish you could walk for ever.

30 October
Holy Island, Northumberland

Everywhere in Northumberland, and not just along the Roman wall, the raw flavour of frontier country hangs in the wind, as distinctive as a Craster kipper. You can sense it among the dunes at Bamburgh, under the hoary old sea castle built by King Ida the Flamebearer; and even more strongly at Lindisfarne Castle on Holy Island, though here the enemy were sixteenth-century Scottish pirates.

Holy Island is time-warp territory: only 60 miles from Newcastle, but for about three hours on either side of high water it can feel as remote as the dark side of the moon. The best approach is through Belford, snug under its ridge of Whin Sill crag, with the Blue Bell Hotel buried in crimson cascades of virginia creeper; and then the immense panorama of dunes and blown sand, white breakers and the strange, half-drowned island beyond, with the castle on its little pinnacle, drawing the eye like some fanciful redoubt in a Renaissance painting.

The nearest mainland village is Beal – in Old English, *Beo-hyll*, the Hill of the Bees – where the monks must have kept their hives, breaking out the sweet combs each year to ease their daily hardships with mead. As you draw closer, coming down over the high ground from Belford, the island itself takes on a flat, rough-hewn shape, like the head of a housecarl's war axe, with its blade set against the sea.

Lindisfarne Castle, Holy Island

I drove out to it over a narrow causeway still wet and smelling of the sea, past glistening sands with sinister names: the Swad; the Slakes. Halfway across stands a box on stilts, a refuge for travellers caught napping by the tide. To the south, stakes mark the line of the Pilgrims' Way, which leads across the sands for three miles from Beal shore to Chare Ends. Inland, rain had begun to fall over the Cheviot Hills. A cold wind came in from the sea, carrying the unearthly crooning voices of eider ducks floating beneath the grassy cliffs of the Heugh.

Seabirds and seals; wild geese in winter; dunes, deeps and shining sands. The austerity of the place must have suited Aidan and his Irish monks who settled here in the seventh century AD to establish the Celtic church and evangelize the north. Then in 793 the marauding Danes came ashore, plundered the church, burnt the abbey and murdered the monks. For another century the threat of the longships hung over the island; and in 875, fearing another invasion, the monks left for good, taking with them their most precious relics, including the bones of St Aidan, St Cuthbert's coffin and the beautiful Lindisfarne Gospels, now in the British Museum.

Today's invaders are a different breed, who plunder nothing but the silence of the dunes and take home bottles of Lindisfarne mead. Summer is busy with visitors. In 1983 nearly fifty thousand people paid to look round Lindisfarne Castle, now managed by the National Trust. But in winter the island is left to itself again, hallowed ground where saints once trod.

All that remains of the early monastery is a collection of pillow stones carved with runes and kept in the Priory Museum.. Also housed in the museum is a remarkable round-headed tombstone said to depict the two faces of Dark Age Northumbria, pagan and Christian: on one

Curlew

side is carved a band of kilted warriors armed with swords and battle axes; the other shows two figures kneeling before the cross. The priory itself is now a ruin. The building was begun by the Normans in 1093, using dark red sandstone shipped from the mainland; but in 1537 it became a victim of the Dissolution and was converted into storehouses for the military garrison.

No doubt some of its stones were stolen to build the castle some ten years later. Perched on top of Beblowe Crag – at 100 feet above the sea the island's highest point – it was conceived as a bulwark against the Scots, was besieged by both sides during the Civil War and occupied briefly by the Jacobites in 1715. In 1819 the garrison finally had its guns withdrawn and the coastguards moved in. The nineteenth century was a time of comparative prosperity for the island, when lime quarrying and the Baltic herring trade were at their peak; but the castle fell into disrepair until it was bought by Edward Hudson, proprietor of *Country Life*. In 1903 Hudson called in the famous architect Sir Edwin Lutyens, who successfully transformed the old Border stronghold into a comfortable country house without destroying its fairytale silhouette. It changed hands twice more before being given to the National Trust in 1944.

I walked up the ramp to the castle entrance. Each shallow step was laid with cobbles in a herringbone pattern, a typical Lutyens touch. Under the walls on the eastern side of the crag stood three black wooden shacks – fishermen's sheds converted from the upturned hulks of herring boats. When the herring fishery failed at the turn of the century, the boats were sawn in half, coated with pitch against the weather and fitted with doors to make snug storehouses.

Inside the castle, light from the mullioned windows gleamed on Flemish oak and walnut furniture, pewter tankards and brass chandeliers, in cold stone rooms with vaulted ceilings. The sea wind roared in the great chimneys with a sound like an approaching tube train. 'Lutyens chimneys are famous for blowing back,' said the Trust warden. 'In here you either freeze or choke.'

From the Upper Battery I looked out across the harbour waters to the shingle bank of Long Rig and the slender twin obelisks on Old Law. They were day marks – navigational aids for the old-time skippers who called to collect cargoes of lime for Dundee or cured herrings for the Baltic. Beyond, to the south, the dunes marched away around a vast curve of sand to the dark, crouching shape of Bamburgh Castle; and out to sea the low, rocky silhouettes of the Farne Islands were strung out in line astern along the eastern horizon: Crumstone, Staple Island, Brownsman, Longstone, Megstone, the Wamses.

Although there was only a moderate swell I could see waves exploding like slow-motion shellbursts against the cliffs. Out there the seals would be moaning in the suck and slap of cold waves, and gulls wailing over whinstone ledges thick with guano.

Seals also frequent the waters around Holy Island, particularly off the north coast, while the surrounding dunes, saltmarsh and mudflats are better known for wildfowl and waders. All these empty shores from Goswick Sands down to Budle Bay form part of a nature reserve of international importance, and winter is when they come into their own. Already the greylag geese had arrived: an advance guard of 500, whose numbers would increase tenfold in a severe winter, dividing their time between the eel-grass beds and the mainland fields of winter corn. Here, too, come the largest wintering herds of whooper swan in England: 500 birds, with maybe 100 Bewick swans as well. They would arrive in November, with thousands of wigeon and other duck, including mallard and shelduck, pintail, scaup and goldeneye. Joining them would be other migrants from the far north: pale-bellied brent geese from Spitzbergen, for whom Lindisfarne is the only regular wintering ground in Britain, and sometimes short-eared owls from Scandinavia, silent hunters of the lonely marshes, flushing clouds of knot and dunlin.

When the Farne lights began to blink in the gathering dusk, it was time to return to the mainland and the twentieth-century comforts of the Linden Hall Hotel at Longhorsley, to hear 'Johnnie Armstrong' played on the Northumbrian small pipes by David Burleigh. Fifteen years a player, Burleigh is also an accomplished pipemaker, turning out a set a week and exporting them to homesick expatriates. Unlike the great Highland bagpipes, which are still basically a fifteenth-century instrument, the Northumbrian pipes with their dry reeds and stopped chanters kept on evolving until about 1800. 'It is,' said piper Burleigh, 'the difference between the Wurlitzer and the harpsichord.'

Oystercatchers

31 October
Chillingham, Northumberland

Where should I go for a lasting image of Northumberland to take home to the south? To the gaunt skeleton of Dunstanburgh Castle, hung about with sea fret on the lonely coast between Boulmer and Beadnell? To Otterburn on the River Rede, where Douglas fought Percy by moonlight in 1388 at the Battle of Chevy Chase, and Douglas fell, to be remembered in the most moving of all Border ballads? Or up the Breamish from Ingram into the Northumberland National Park to Linhope Spout or Bloodybush Edge? In the end I settled for none of these, but set out instead to see the wild white cattle of Chillingham.

No one knows the exact origins of these extraordinary animals, but they are truly wild, as wild as the fallow deer which run with them in the 300 acres of parkland oaks and soft, rushy meadows at Chillingham Castle, and as fierce as the day when Thomas Bewick made his famous woodcut of the king bull. The shape of the skull and the peculiar set of the high, crescent horns have led experts to believe they could be direct descendants of the aurochs or wild ox, *Bos primigenius*, which roamed the forests of Bronze Age Britain and survived in Poland until as late as the seventeenth-century. What is beyond dispute is that a pure-bred herd has lived here in Northumberland since at least 1220, when Henry III gave permission for the castle of Chillingham to be 'castellated and crenellated' and its grounds emparked within a high stone wall. Since then they have remained uncrossed with any domestic cattle; and in all that time they have never produced a calf that was anything but white.

'Splendid beasts,' said Fred Allen, the park warden, as we climbed the steep, wooded track from the park entrance. 'I love them with a great affection.' Seven years ago he was a driving instructor. Before that he had spent most of his working life in a North Shields factory. Now, as the guardian of the Chillingham herd, he seemed the most contented of men.

We crossed a meadow and entered a gate where a burn trickled down the valley. On the other side a peaceful panorama of rough grass and oak glades spread away towards a brow of rusted bracken with crags breaking through, and a crest of pines. Almost at once a bull strolled out of the trees and began to rub his neck and flanks against an alder. We gave him a wide berth and walked across the clearing to where a group of cows were resting under the oaks, chewing cud. When we came within 50 yards of them they stood up and stared at us suspiciously, then slowly moved deeper into the woods.

One of the many mysteries surrounding the Chillingham cattle is how they have managed to interbreed for seven centuries without any apparent ill effects. The clue to their remarkable survival may lie in the natural hierarchy which exists within the herd, for only the fittest and strongest bull sires calves. As the dominant male he is the king bull and allows no other bull to mate with any of the cows. Sometimes a younger bull, eager to mate and feeling his growing strength, will step out from the herd to paw the ground and blare his challenge at the king. If the king bull accepts, he, too, will advance and go through the same ritual of pawing and bellowing, until one or the other suddenly attacks. Such fights are brief and seldom result in serious injury. Only three bulls have been killed in the past fifty years; but the loser invariably moves away from the herd to live in temporary exile, becoming irritable and very dangerous to approach.

Since the First World War the strength of the herd has remained fairly stable at between thirty-five and forty animals. They seldom suffer from infectious or contagious illness, and may be resistant even to foot and mouth disease, which came within two miles of Chillingham when a major outbreak swept across Northumberland in 1967. The biggest catastrophe the herd has suffered in recent times happened in the severe winter of 1947. Hay was scarce. There had been a drought the previous year, followed by torrential rains at harvest time, so that when the blizzards struck Chillingham there was hardly any fodder. All roads were blocked and the park was buried by snowdrifts up to 40 feet deep. When rescuers eventually fought their way through, bringing bales of oat straw on the back of a carthorse, the cattle were so hungry that the older and stronger animals would not share the fodder but drove the younger and weaker ones away. In January, when the blizzards began, the Chillingham herd was thirty-three strong. In March, when the snow cleared, only thirteen animals were left, and not one of them was a youngster.

Chillingham bull

The afternoon passed too quickly. We retraced our steps and found that down by the burn the bull was still rubbing himself against the tree. His winter coat had begun to grow; during November it would grow even thicker, and he would not shed it until April. He looked magnificent: straight-backed, and with a tight, curly fleece around the boss of his horns. I asked Fred Allen if he had ever been chased by a bull. 'Aye, it happens,' he said. 'They can weigh ten hundredweight, but my word they're nimble.'

A cold wind hissed over the meadow. The distant summits of the Cheviots were still bathed in sunshine, but low clouds were now scudding down from the north. If it snowed, the cattle would shelter in the woods. Used to hard weather, they would not go under cover even if barns were provided. They had not changed in seven hundred years, and were as wild now as their ancestors had been when the park was first enclosed. The bull watched us as we crossed the burn, and his black nostrils wrinkled as he caught our scent. I hoped the winter would not be too severe for him.

NOVEMBER

2 November

The Border Country

I came over the Tweed by night, like the cattle-rustling reivers of old, the landscape a mystery beyond Berwick, wrapped in darkness, not to be opened until morning. When daylight came, and a breakfast of black pudding and bacon rashers at the Chirnside Countryhouse Hotel, I set eyes for the first time on the prosperous farmlands of the Merse, the wide, rolling fields, sleek earth freshly ploughed, looking back into England at the dim and distant hulks of the Cheviots.

The Scottish Borders are as empty as the sea. You could cram the entire population into Wembley Stadium and still have room to spare. Once across the Tweed the fetch of the land is a slow, northward surge of haugh and law, pasture and plough, long ridges plumed with trees, and here and there a sullen summit, hinting at grander heights to come.

So peaceful now, yet never was a land so cruelly fought over: there is hardly an inch that was not once drenched in the blood of its feuding families, or which has not echoed to the hoofbeats of wild night riders and vengeful armies bent on hacking each other to bits in the lonely mosses. That was four hundred years ago, when the Scottish Marches were as lawless as the Khyber Pass, when the bale fires flickered their beacon warnings and the Border reivers – Scotts, Elliots, Kerrs, Armstrongs – rode out with their steel bonnets and long lances to lift each other's cattle. The map is scattered with names that ring like battle cries: Blackhope Scar, Scabcleuch Hill, Piper's Knowe, Slain Men's Lea. Even today the hills and valleys reek of Border balladry. You can sense it, if you have a nose for such things, at Smailholm Tower, a Border pele as stark as a tombstone, reached by a road that runs through a farmyard; and nowhere is it stronger than under the sinister walls of Hermitage Castle, skulking in the western fells at the approaches to Liddesdale – once the bloodiest valley in Britain.

Now the reivers and their turbulent way of life – which added the terms 'blackmail' and 'red-handed' to the English language – are no more than a folk memory. But some things never change. The salmon still follow the silver Tweed deep into the plunging hills, past Sir Walter Scott's favourite view at Bemersyde, the ruined abbeys of Dryburgh and Melrose, and Scott's own house at Abbotsford. And every autumn, when the salmon are running and this loveliest of British rivers is lit by the smouldering colours of the turning trees, every pool holds the solemn figures of salmon fishermen, silent at their devotions.

In Peebles, I asked Ian Fraser, who runs one of the best tackle shops in the Borders, why people pay hundreds of pounds to stand up to their armpits for day after day in the Tweed's chill waters. At first he looked surprised, as if I had uttered some unexpected blasphemy. Then he leaned over his counter and tugged me sharply by the lapels. 'The take, laddie, it's the take,' he said. 'The magic moment when the fish is on and the adrenalin is pumping and you forget the cold and how long you have been flogging the river.'

The Tweed isn't what it was, says Fraser: too many netsmen at the

Salmon

mouth of the river; too many Faroese skippers fishing the salmon's Atlantic feeding grounds. Yet the autumn run is still impressive; and, as if to make the point, only yesterday he had slipped out of his shop and killed two fish in an hour.

The herring, too, no longer come to the Berwickshire coast as they once did, when the women of Eyemouth 'travelled the herring' each summer, following the shoals from Yarmouth to Shetland, sometimes sleeping three to a hut and carrying their own beds filled with chaff. The museum in Eyemouth recalls those days, and one day more terrible than all the rest – 14 October 1881 – when a great storm struck the fishing fleet. Of the 45 boats and 279 fishermen which had put to sea, only 26 vessels and 150 men returned, leaving 73 widows and 263 fatherless children.

Mine was a fleeting visit – much too short to do justice to the full measure of the Borders, but long enough for the essence of the place to distil itself in a series of indelible memories. I remember the majestic avenues of Mellerstain, which give the lie to the English belief that Scotland is a treeless country, and the cold rooms of Traquair, where history seeps out of the walls like damp – a house visited by twenty-seven kings and still lived in after nine hundred years. If I close my eyes it takes no great effort of will to recall the drystone dykes and wind-blown crows, and the endless hills of autumn grass on the road to Carter Bar. I remember the sound of the burns in spate, and the bleating of sheep in the sharp upland air as I watched a shepherd and his two dogs working the fells above Talla. And best of all was Scott's View, with the sun going down behind the unearthly summits of the Eildons and the Tweed glittering like chain mail in its wooded hollows. And, as I watched, a salmon flung itself from the river, a gleaming slab of silver that hung slowly in the air, or so it seemed, then fell back with a great splash and sank beneath the ripples.

5 November
Powerstock, Dorset

For days a Guy Fawkes bonfire had been taking shape in the old vicarage garden. What had begun as a modest pile of dead brushwood and garden trimmings was now a towering pyramid of planks and timbers, old doors, newspapers, broken furniture, worn-out car tyres and even a small tree. Now fireworks night was here, and the whole village had come to see the bonfire and its scarecrow effigy burned.

Someone stepped forward with a box of matches. At first the kindling only smouldered in the damp night air; but soon small tongues of flame took hold inside the pyre. They spread quickly, licking hungrily along the drier timbers which spat and cracked as they caught, until the entire structure was ablaze. There was no wind. The red sparks flew upwards in a pillar of smoke and the flames grew even taller, lighting up the circle of watching faces.

Then the fireworks began. Roman candles hissed like vipers in the wet grass, erupting in fountains of furry gold and silver sparks. Others threw up shellbursts of eerie red and green flares that fell soundlessly through the dark. Whizzbangs and thunderflashes filled the air with acrid gunpowder smells. Catherine wheels shrieked on wooden posts and rockets rushed skywards, to explode with a crackle of dazzling stars that drew gasps of delight from the upturned faces.

Afterwards, when the fire had collapsed in a glow of embers, and the last rocket had reverberated among the surrounding combes, there were beer and cider on trestle tables, hot dogs and spit-roasted lamb, while children hunted for spent fireworks in the grass and a tawny owl's quavering cry floated softly down the valley.

To me the fifth of November has always been one of those symbolic festivals like Christmas and Easter which measure the passing seasons. For just as our pagan ancestors once lit Hallowe'en fires to rekindle the dying sun, so Guy Fawkes Night is much more than a celebration of gunpowder, treason and plot. The long nights have come, and the first frosts. Now the fireworks are over. Autumn has been consigned to the flames. The leaves are down. Winter is coming.

7 November
Lewesdon, Dorset

The highest hill in Dorset is Pilsdon Pen. From the Iron Age camp on its breezy summit, almost a thousand feet above the sea, the fields fall away to the old flax hayes and heavy clay lowlands of the Marshwood Vale, with the Charmouth cliffs beyond. On a fine day the sea views are unsurpassed – the whole of Lyme Bay glittering to the south, from Portland Bill to Beer Head and away down past Teignmouth in wash on wash of receding blue to the faint pencil line of Start Point on the western horizon.

A mile and a half to the east of Pilsdon looms another great hill: Lewesdon. Viewed from the sea, these twin eminences have been familiar day marks for generations of mackerel fishermen, and are still known to the boatmen of West Bay as the Cow and Calf. Seen from so great a distance, it would be hard to say which hill was bigger; for there is no more than 15 feet in height between them. But while Pilsdon stands bare against the sky, Lewesdon is covered from head to foot in shaggy woods.

Compared to Surrey, where I was born, Dorset is not a woodland county. I miss the solace of long winter walks through Hurt Wood, the Spanish chestnuts of Albury Park, the lofty beeches of Ranmore and Holmbury; and never more so than now, in the bittersweet days of early November when the colours of the dying leaves are at their most intense. That is why, every year, it has become a family tradition to visit the beechwoods of Lewesdon.

The first clump of beeches overhanging the lane had already been stripped bare, and we feared we had come too late; but higher up, as we toiled up the old, steep track to the summit, we found Lewesdon as I had hoped: the wood fallen silent, waiting for winter, the aisles of beeches still thick with leaves. There was no sun to light them. Instead the leaves seemed to give out their own pure radiance, piercing the wood's grey shadows with sharp russet and rich tawny gleams.

We walked on, wading through carpets of fallen leaves. Mosses lay in vivid green cushions along the medieval woodland banks, and fungi had burst through the leaf litter. There were several different species, but I could recognize only the poisonous common earthball, the sweaty red caps of a toadstool aptly known as the sickener, and the yellowish, fan-shaped tiers of the giant polypore sprouting from the base of a decaying trunk. Mixed with the earthy taint of rotting leaves, their damp underworld odours clung to the nostrils: the ineluctable smell of autumn.

Halfway up the hill lies a boggy hollow which is normally a place of rainwater pools and loose mats of floating sweet-grass, but this year it held nothing but a mass of leaves. We pushed through a clearing of waist-high bracken to the summit, where Scots pines stand in a dark crest. I stood on the ridge and looked down through the trees where mist was congealing in the November dusk. Somewhere down there lay the Marshwood Vale. It is witchcraft country, or so the stories would have you believe: a perfect setting for Bettiscombe Manor and its legend of the screaming skull. Even today it is an oddly secretive corner of England, one of the last places where Dorset Blue Vinney cheese was made, accessible only by skulking lanes that sneak through the fields like rabbit runs from one hamlet to the next, past streams and nightingale spinneys and meadows where wild daffodils bloom.

OVERLEAF: *Autumn in Wyre Forest*

Woodland fungi

43

Wyre Forest — 10.00 —
November 10/83 14.30 hrs.

Down in the wood a heavy silence clung to the trees; but, with the onset of dusk, wrens began to tick and blackbirds chinked in alarm as a tawny owl began to call. The air, which had been still all day, was stirring. A breeze was coming in from the sea, and as we made our way back down the hill I could hear it soughing in the tops of the pines on the ridge. Soon the wind was all around us, gusting stronger by the minute, until we were walking in a maelstrom of falling leaves.

9 November
Wyre Forest, Hereford and Worcester

We entered the forest along a railway track: when it was opened, in 1861, the line ran from Bewdley to Tenbury Wells, but now it is deserted. Axed by Beeching a century later almost to the day, it has become a natural forest ride, banks and cuttings bearded with willow-herb, splashed crimson with wild rose hips. The woods have closed in, reclaiming their own.

Wyre Forest is a miraculous survival: an old English wood only 12 miles from the industrial sprawl of the west Midlands. It is one of our last great tracts of ancient semi-natural woodland; yet compared with the New Forest, Epping or Savernake it is a strangely secret place. It straddles the Hereford and Worcester/Shropshire border, which is here marked by the Dowles Brook, a tributary of the River Severn, and has been wooded at least since early Saxon times.

Brought under forest laws after the Conquest, it later became a royal chase for Plantagenet and Tudor monarchs who hunted fallow deer from Tickenhall Palace. Today you can walk five miles in any direction from the middle of the forest and still be surrounded by trees. A lot of the old broad-leaved canopy has been felled by the Forestry Commission and replaced with conifers; but the 900 acres managed as a national nature reserve by the Nature Conservancy Council still represents one of the largest surviving areas of native woodland in Britain.

Here in the heartland, oak is king. Two species flourish: the common or pedunculate oak, *Quercus robur*, with its long-stemmed acorns and stalkless leaves, grows in the damp valley bottoms; and the durmast or sessile oak, *Quercus petraea*, recognized by its stemless acorns and long-stalked leaves, favours the acid soils of the slopes and hillsides. In Wyre Forest the durmast oak is the dominant species.

The oaks are uniformly tall, yet few have a trunk thicker than a man's body. There are no New Forest giants here; no gnarled and ancient pollards. For centuries the oaks of Wyre were coppiced – constantly cut down to encourage new growth from the base or stool – to make charcoal for the smelting of Black Country iron, so they were never allowed to grow too old before being thrown. Nor will you find many maiden oaks, self-sown from fallen acorns. The trees are mostly offshoots from old coppiced stools, recognizable by the pronounced kink at the base of each trunk where it emerged as a lateral bud from the parent stump.

So many oaks, so many shades of brown. Wyre in autumn is a magical place of banks and dells and boggy hollows, of brooks in deep valleys, green moss underfoot and glades of bracken, not rusted this year but bleached to a pale, ethereal yellow. Beyond the track, where the trees sloped away into shadowy silence, the day dissolved in a drizzle of leaves.

My guide to this enchanted forest was John Robinson, the reserve's senior warden, who lives with his wife and two children in an idyllic woodland cottage. His was the home of a true naturalist. There was a pet weasel in the garage and an injured tawny owl in a cage. But Robinson is no sentimentalist. Only two days ago he had shot a mink on his bird table. Now, teeth set in an evil grin, it dangled from the wire of his chicken run. Feral mink were a problem, he told me. Dippers, wagtails and water voles were all scarcer since the mink had established themselves along the Dowles Brook.

We walked through a succession of relic coppices: Cold Harbour, Lord's Yard, Shelf Held Coppice. In summer, said Robinson, there were wood warblers and redstarts. Adders basked in the dry, stony places. Clouds of silver-washed fritillaries haunted the woodland rides, and the beautiful banded agrion damselfly could be found along the streams. Once, too, the Kentish glory flew here, a handsome white and chestnut moth whose caterpillers fed on birch leaves. Wyre was its last *Woodcock* English stronghold. Now it had gone. Collectors helped it to extinction by the method of capture known as 'assembling': a captive-bred female moth would be hung from a tree in a muslin bag, where it would emit pheromones to lure in all the nearby males.

Deep in the forest a jay screamed – a harsh sound, like tearing linen. There have been many jays this year. All over Europe, thanks to a small parasitic gall wasp, the acorn crop has failed. In southern England there is hardly an acorn to be found, and the hungry jays – some have flocked from as far as Poland and Scandinavia – have been scouring the country.

Farther on we startled a woodcock; or rather, it startled us, so suddenly did it clatter away from beneath our feet. Its mottled plumage had been a perfect match for the colours of the fallen oak leaves. What a

mysterious bird it is, larger than a snipe but with the same zigzag flight; a woodland wraith, hiding under the trees by day and emerging at dusk to probe for worms in ditches and boggy hollows.

Towards midday the haze dispersed, and the sun came through to light the yellow birches. There was no movement of air, yet the leaves continued to fall, slowly turning, to gather in drifts under the trees. Occasionally we passed a guelder rose, its berries glassy red in heavy drooping clusters. Beech trees glowed amber against the light. Always there was oak, but in places the gean or wild cherry grew, and the native British small-leaved lime. At one spot we found a wild service tree, another ancient woodland species but scarce even here. Its leaves are similar in shape to those of the field maple, and their autumn colour is a deep, lambent bronze. The tree's curious name is probably an Old English corruption of the name the Romans gave to it, *Sorbus*. Its greenish brown fruits, which resemble large haws, can be eaten like medlars if kept until November.

The most famous tree that ever grew in Wyre Forest was a relative of the service tree, the celebrated Whitty Pear, *Sorbus pyriformis*. Its history is well documented: the earliest record, dated 1678, describes its fruit as being *'in September so rough as to be ready to strangle one; but being then gathered, and kept till October they eat as well as any medlar'*. Even in the seventeenth century the Whitty Pear was considered to be a veteran; yet it survived as a decrepit hulk until as late as 1862 when it was burned down by vandals. Luckily two descendants of the legendary tree, grown either as grafts or from seed, continued to flourish at Arley Castle, and it was one of these which produced the 'direct descendant' which was planted to replace the original Whitty Pear in 1913. Then it was a slender five-foot sapling. Now it is more than 50 feet tall and even bigger than the original. The bark is rough, the leaves not unlike those of mountain ash, and the fruit are like small pears. It is a fascinating story but it leaves one mystery unexplained: how did this rare tree, a native of Asia Minor, come to be growing in an ancient English forest in the middle of the seventeenth century?

Elsewhere in the forest there is also a scattering of yews. Some people believe they were left because symbolic significance has been attached to yews since pagan times and it was considered unlucky to cut them down; but in truth they owe their survival to a more practical reason. When the forest was cut for coppice wood the charcoal burners used them as shelters to keep their timber dry. They simply stacked their logs under the ready-made awning of the living yew, whose dense foliage would keep off all but the heaviest of downpours.

We came to a clearing where a circle of bracken surrounded a vague raised mound of brambles – the site of a charcoal burner's hearth. There were many such spots in the forest, said John Robinson. Dig deep enough and the earth would still be black from the long-cold fires. Once Bewdley lived off the forest, and its coppiced oaks seemed inexhaustible. There was wood for the charcoal burners and peeled bark for the tanners. Nothing was wasted – even the sawdust was used for the floors of pubs and butchers' shops. But charcoal burning came ·to an end around the turn of the century. Coppicing ceased and the woods fell silent. Now only the wine red leaves of the brambles glowed like embers over the forgotten hearth.

Today history has come full circle. The woods are again being coppiced, but this time the purpose is conservation. Robinson showed me where he had ring-barked some oaks to provide dead standing timber for woodpeckers, and felled others to create a clearing for woodland flowers and butterflies. In another clearing all the oaks had been newly coppiced, leaving only the stumps from which new poles would spring.

Most of the felled oaks were between fifty and eighty years old. Already their limbs had been lopped off, and now the craggy grey-green trunks lay stacked at the edge of the clearing, waiting for the wedge and the bandsaw. 'A commercial forester would probably let them grow bigger, but we're felling for conservation,' said Robinson. 'There are plenty of oaks to grow on to old age, but we need to encourage more young trees if we are to keep tomorrow's forest in good shape.' We crouched over a sawn stump to count the growth rings. Here was a life laid bare – a section through history, measured in circles. There were sixty-nine rings: one for each summer since its first bud opened in the year the First World War began. Some rings had wider gaps between them: these were the good wet years when the tree had done well, said Robinson; the thin, close rings represented the dry years, when growth had been slow.

Nowadays Wyre oak has no great value, for it is too susceptible to heart and butt rot, legacies inherited from the old coppiced stools. Such timber is known as 'stub oak', and most of it goes for fence posts, although sound trunks may be squared off to make sturdy gateposts for around £18 apiece. One of the woodmen employed to take out the timber showed his skill at cleaving the oak into suitable lengths for fence posts. Like all country crafts it looked deceptively simple and was beautiful to watch in its economy of effort. Three heavy iron wedges were inserted, one at a time; then three sledgehammer blows and the job was done.

Grey squirrels cause some damage in the forest, but deer are a bigger

problem. Their fondness for young shoots and seedlings makes it harder for the woods to regenerate. Only when the young trees are protected by brambles do they escape, for the deer are lazy and like to follow the same forest paths. Wyre has always been renowned for its fallow deer. We had seen one earlier in the day, a fine buck with a dark coat and wide-spreading antlers, stepping soundlessly across the path ahead of us. But he would have been nothing compared to the Great Buck of Wyre – a beast of extraordinary size who carried the biggest antlers in living memory. When he was shot by a Forestry Commission marksman in November 1965 he was found to have been almost totally blind.

The shyest creature in the forest is the dormouse, a nocturnal denizen of the hazel understorey. It is an animal of southern Britain, but nowhere is it common. In summer it builds its domed nest among the spiny green stems of dog roses: a tight grapefruit-sized ball of honeysuckle bark, moss and oak leaves. But in October the dormouse goes to ground under the fallen leaves and old hazel coppice roots. There it will remain until April, curled up against the cold – a true hibernator, its body clock slowed to an almost imperceptible tick. Once, said John Robinson, he had found one in a long-tailed tit's nest. Instinctively he had tried to catch it, but it had popped out of his hands 'like a wet bar of soap'.

The day was drawing to a close. Mist was returning and the shadows had begun to thicken where the slanting sun no longer penetrated; but the forest still had one more secret to reveal. Back at the Dowles Brook, Robinson began to search under the foot-long slabs of rock that littered the shallows. Here lived fingerling trout and stone loach, eels, lampreys and miller's thumbs. Even salmon came to spawn in this modest tributary of the Severn; but Robinson sought none of these. Once more he bent to lift a stone. A fog of sediment arose. When it cleared he made a sudden grab, then triumphantly held his arm aloft. There, squirming in his fist, was a freshwater crayfish.

In Britain, wild crayfish are no longer common; disease and pollution have greatly reduced their numbers. This was the first I had seen in this country since I was ten years old. Its stubby scorpion body, encased in opaque, brownish green armour, was about three inches long. Held between thumb and forefinger it waved its pincers like a shadow boxer, trying in vain to nip my hand. Carefully I returned it to the water by the stone beneath which it had been hiding. For a moment it did not move. Then came a sudden swirl in the sediment, leaving only the water flowing and a drifting carpet of yellow leaves.

Freshwater crayfish

14 November
Exe Estuary, Devon

Dawlish Warren had closed for winter. The go-kart track was deserted, the beach huts were padlocked, and the whole place had the derelict, slightly tawdry atmosphere of the English seaside out of season. But out beyond the last hutments lay a wilder, cleaner world of windswept dunes where gulls screamed over thunderous seas and sanderlings scurried at the tide's edge.

The Warren is a gigantic sandbar stretching towards Exmouth for one and a half miles across the Exe estuary. The Outer Warren is a line of seaward-facing sandhills bristling with marram-grass and protected in places by stone-filled cages. Behind the dunes lies a wilderness of sallow, phragmites and flooded slacks known as Greenland Lake. It was once a tidal lagoon, formed in the 1860s when a dam was built across the end by the Exe Bight Oyster Fishing and Pier Company; but in 1869 the dam was overwhelmed by a storm and the oysters smothered by sand. Now it shelters a wealth of wild plants, among them the Warren crocus, found nowhere else in mainland Britain.

I walked out past the golf course to the birdwatchers' hide. The path wanders behind the dunes over acres of rabbit-nibbled turf whose summer flowers had long since withered. Dead seedheads of evening primrose rattled in the sea wind, and dunnocks sought refuge among the hairy stems of burnet rose. On the sandflats of Bight Marsh a flock of linnets were foraging for glasswort seeds between yellowing stretches of cord-grass, and did not fly up as I walked past.

The hide stands on the edge of the Inner Warren, looking up the estuary towards the yachts and trawlers lying at their moorings under the red Devon fields. It was a relief to go inside out of the penetrating wind. I peered out through the slit windows to find the shoreline packed with waders – high water had forced them back until they were huddled in dense, twittering packs. Most numerous were the oyster-catchers, smartly dressed in black and white, feathers puffed out against the cold and every bird facing into the eye of the wind. Other birds moved among them: a herd of knot, droves of dunlin, scatterings of curlew, bar-tailed godwit and grey plover.

The oystercatchers were waiting for the tide to turn. As soon as the water receded they would fly to the sandbar known as Bull Hill to feed on the glistening mussel beds, hammering open the tough shells with their coral red bills. Every day they would consume the equivalent of

OVERLEAF: *Exe estuary from Dawlish Warren, Devon*

51

three quarters of their body weight in bivalves, each bird eating as many as a hundred mussels. Most oystercatchers on the Exe estuary are adults: that is to say, birds over four years old. The few hundred which remain in the breeding season are immature. The rest begin to arrive towards the end of August, pouring south from their breeding haunts in Scotland, Norway and the Netherlands to winter in noisy flocks up to 3500 strong. Add maybe 17,000 other shorebirds (dunlin, curlew, redshank, turnstone) and more than 10,000 wintering wildfowl, and the importance of these rich feeding grounds becomes apparent.

Imperceptibly at first, the tide began to drop. Mingled smells of mud and seaweed hung about the hide. Occasionally the roar of a diesel would echo across the water from the railway line which hugs the estuary between Exeter and Dawlish. Quicksilver knot flew up in alarm, dashing this way and that in perfect unison like a shoal of fish. I looked for a predator – peregrine or short-eared owl – but saw none; and the zigzagging flock swirled to rest in a haze of flickering wings farther down the saltmarsh.

All life in the estuary moves to the twice-daily pulse of the tide. Brent geese which had been floating in small, grunting groups far out in the roadsteads now came winging in to the shallows to dibble for eel-grass. This is an important stronghold for the dark-bellied brents, who migrate from Arctic Russia to winter here. The first birds usually arrive in early October and build up to a peak of perhaps 3000 or more in December and January. So far, according to the latest tally posted in the hide, 254 brent geese had arrived, of which 15 now stood in full view, easy to recognize by their sooty heads and stubby beaks.

Not all the seafood of the Exe is eaten by the birds. At lunchtime I drove up the estuary to Cockwood (which the locals pronounce 'Cock'ood'). Behind the railway line, which here runs along the sea wall, a muddy creek forms a small harbour with a couple of pubs. The day's menu at the Ship offered fresh local crabs and cockles, and mussels cooked in garlic butter.

An hour later, back at the hide, the tide was falling fast. Acres of wet mud and sand now lay exposed, but the oystercatchers had not yet moved. They were still waiting for the outgoing flood to expose the mussel beds in midstream. As the estuary emptied and its waters shrank between the sands, the skies filled with rushing wings as birds moved between Bight Marsh and the rich feeding grounds of Cockle Sand on the Exmouth shore. Wigeon whistled down the wind. More brents arrived in small family groups, unsettling the fast, flitting dunlin. Three turnstones were running over the mud, rooting for crustaceans in a flotsam of seaweed. A curlew stalked deliberately

Redshank

through the cord-grass, then flew out over the water with a wild, bubbling cry, unbearably sad and broken-voiced.

In late afternoon sunlight the estuary was a cold, sharp blue which stood out in vivid contrast against the red Devon ploughlands. Offshore to the east a small raft of duck caught my eye. They were mergansers, saw-billed duck from northern Britain. They swam low in the water, like cormorants, the males very handsome in their new winter plumage, with dark green heads, white throats and rich chestnut breasts.

I walked back through the dunes and out to the shore where shells scrunched underfoot between battered wooden groynes. The day was drawing to a close. Against the sun the tips of the marram looked like molten glass, and the feathery tops of the phragmites shone silver and yellow, like a barn owl's feathers. Overrun in summer, the Warren in winter is a lonely place, shriven by the wind, returned to the wild. When at last the sun slid down, it left an apple green cupola of sky filled with black skeins of duck and roosting gulls. All cloud had gone. There would be frost tonight.

At Powderham, beneath the castle walls, I saw from the car fallow deer grazing under parkland oaks; their antlered heads stared from the shadows. At Exeter it was almost dark. Out in the estuary the oystercatchers would be feeding now, falling on Bull Hill in shrilling

Brent geese

droves, jabbing and hacking at the blue-black mussels until the turning tide drove them back once more to Bight Marsh.

19 November
Askerswell, Dorset

The village of Askerswell is only a couple of miles from my home, but to reach it I have to cross one of England's great geological divides, climbing out of the greensand country around Powerstock towards the great gable end of Eggardon, where the chalk begins. A friend of mine has a farm on the other side of the hill, not far from the spot where the little River Asker bubbles from the chalk to trickle down a valley choked with wild cress and alder carr: a good place to walk in winter.

We forded the Asker just short of its source, where it is still narrow enough to leap. As we squelched through the mud on the other side into a mossy chaos of wind-thrown timber we put up a fine roe buck, which bounced away into the wood. Eventually we found a footpath filled with leaves: an old, hollow way burrowing through the trees to the high chalk slopes above. It was, said my farmer friend, a smugglers' track, one of many in this part of Dorset, where contraband landed at night on the lonely Chesil Bank was run ashore and carried inland by pack train towards the towns of Somerset. It is no coincidence that the nearest pub is called Spyways. Nor was there any doubting the path's ancient lineage. It follows an old parish boundary, marked by a bank on which crouched some of the most grotesque and misshapen trees I have ever seen. Most were ash, though there was also some hazel, now derelict and rotting. Centuries of coppicing and plashing had transformed them into hedgerow hulks, hollowed and arthritic. Yet still they clung to life, each spring putting out the leaves which now lay in yellow heaps around our feet.

Above the woods we circled a grassy downland combe, then struck out across bare, flinty fields beside a straggling thorn hedge. Far out in the emptiness of the ploughlands four roe deer were nibbling the young winter corn; but long before we had left the scant shelter of the hedge they had bounded away in line astern to vanish into the combe.

It is odd that, unlike their larger and more statuesque relatives, the fallow, roe deer have never been seriously considered as beasts of the chase. Northern Britain is their stronghold. In the south their numbers declined after the Middle Ages until by the eighteenth century they were almost extinct, surviving in only a few favoured localities such as Cranborne Chase in Dorset. There the fugitive roe clung on, hardy little outlaws used to living off the land and evading their enemies. Meanwhile, others remained emparked at Petworth in Sussex, where their dwindling numbers were strengthened with fresh blood from the Duke of Buccleuch's estate in Scotland; and in 1800 Lord Dorchester introduced roe deer at Milton Abbas in Dorset. It was from these two aristocratic bridgeheads that the roe deer broke out to begin their remarkable recolonization of southern England.

Roe deer are true woodland animals, and the Forestry Commission's new conifer plantations have undoubtedly aided their advance, enabling them to fan out eastwards across Surrey into Kent, and westwards deep into Devon, with great numbers in Dorset and Hampshire. Unlike fallow deer, which prefer grass, roe are browsing animals and are most active at dawn and dusk, feeding on tender young tree shoots, shrubs and brambles. In summer their coats are a rich foxy red, in winter a thick donkey brown, lightly frosted with greyer guard hairs. By day they keep to the woods, lying up in dense bramble castles or patches of bracken. Often the only glimpse of a roe deer is the sudden flash of its bold white rump as it bounds off through the trees. The rut takes place in summer, and a resident buck will normally live with one doe as a pair, keeping to his chosen territory which he will defend against other males. The short, spiky antlers are wickedly sharp, and the bucks fight with great savagery, sometimes even to the death.

Dusk was now coming down fast. Partridges began to call. On the roof of the downs, in the middle of a ploughed field, a bulldozer was at work. Backwards and forwards it churned, grinding flints beneath its tracks. The stink of diesel hung in the air. The driver had been working all day, demolishing a prehistoric barrow. Now the job was almost done, the mound almost levelled. Only a rough circle of flint and chalk, paler than the surrounding soil, would be left to tell future generations that a grave had once stood here. Overhead, rooks were flying to their roosts. Their parched voices rasped in the gloom, as if in protest for the Bronze Age chieftain whose dust was being so callously exhumed.

For naturalists as well as archaeologists the destruction of the downlands is a tragedy. In just four decades the great sheepwalks that Thomas Hardy knew have almost vanished. In his day the downs ran in smooth, grassy crests like a rising sea before the wind. From Cranborne Chase to Eggardon they rolled with hardly a blemish: *Roe deer* Hambledon, Hod Hill, Batcombe, Bulbarrow. Constellations of grazing sheep shone like stars on their smooth flanks, and in summer every fold and combe was strewn with the flowers of the high chalk.

Alas, modern farming technology and the need to produce more food brought about a radical change from sheep to arable farming, and the downs were skinned alive. Today, stripped of their thin, green rug, they lie bare all winter long until the barley hides their flinty carcasses. Of the 70,000 acres of ancient turf that were Dorset's crowning glory a century ago, fewer than 5000 scattered acres remain. The rest have been ploughed away in a process which began during the last war and was hastened during the fifties and sixties with the aid of government grants.

It is no use berating the farmers – not when barley is a safer bet than lamb. Besides, the new landscapes are not without a beauty of their own; and never more so than in winter when the chalky ploughlands sprawl about the vales like Siamese cats, creamy and cloud-dappled. No: the chalkland tragedy is not that so much of the Hardy country has gone under the plough; the real sadness stems from a society so indifferent to its past that it allowed the greater part of our downlands to be dismantled with hardly a murmur of dissent. As it is, not even the greatest prehistoric hillforts, as remarkable in their own way as Stonehenge or the Pyramids, have survived unscathed.

We walked on through a gate and across more fresh furrows which had uncovered a desolation of stones and flints, some the size of human

skulls. The ground was very dry, and the flints underfoot gave out a hard, metallic ring. As we continued, we could see that all the high ground on this side of the Roman road had been ploughed. Only in the steep curves and hollows of the plunging combes had the old turf escaped. Too hazardous to plough, it fell away in a tawny staircase of narrow terraces, trodden by generations of grazing sheep. In the valley below, a little owl began to yelp at the dark.

By day these high chalklands are cowed by the marching shapes of giant pylons carrying the National Grid westward across the Marshwood Vale. But when darkness comes, pylons and power lines fade from sight and the downs withdraw once more into an older silence, returning to a past which is never far away on the haunted skylines of the Roman road.

Beyond Askerswell a distant stream of traffic glittered against the night sky where the A35 dual carriageway crosses the downs on its way to Bridport; but soon the lights were lost to view as we dropped down to my friend's farmhouse, to an open fire of sawn elm logs and a brace of pheasant for supper.

30 November

Powerstock, Dorset

The barn owl that frequented the dead-end combe beyond Castle Mill Farm in the autumn had forsaken his old hunting ground. Now, in the dead of winter, he had taken up residence on the rough hillsides beneath Eggardon, drifting over the fields at dusk, quartering the ground as diligently as a harrier. I saw him again on my way home tonight: a ghostly hunter designed for darkness. Perched on a fence post at the side of the road, he stayed long enough for me to see quite clearly the heart-shaped facial mask, the oriental almond eyes, the pearly-king spangles on his buff-mantled shoulders.

The barn owl has always been one of my favourite birds – all the more so because its mysterious presence epitomizes for me the strange and secretive Dorset countryside. In summer other birds come to mind: cuckoos calling when the woods are rank with wild garlic; greenfinches wheezing on laneside wires in the noonday warmth; grasshopper warblers skulking and reeling in the sallow jangles and valley bottoms. But as soon as the frost settles and the bracken dies, when gales roar in to strip the oaks and sea mists shawl the folded combes, then Dorset reverts to its pagan past, and the white barn owl becomes the true spirit of the land in winter, an eloquent emblem for all the tangled country between Eggardon and the Marshwood Vale.

It may well have been the same bird that I had watched in the autumn, for barn owls have become scarce in recent years. Numbers have halved since the war, with the rate of decline nose-diving even more steeply over the past decade. In the 1930s England and Wales alone could claim 12,000 breeding pairs. Today the entire population for Britain and Ireland is probably less than 4000 pairs. Hard winters kill them, for the species is on the edge of its range in Britain, and those in Scotland may be the most northerly barn owls in the world. Overhead wires and poisoned rats also take their toll, as do water butts, in which young owls sometimes drown while bathing. The barn owl is the farmer's friend, a dedicated killer of small rodents.

The intensification of agriculture since the Second World War has swept away much of the old meadowland, hedgerows and rough pasture which harboured the barn owl's prey. The result has been a vicious spiral. Fewer voles means fewer owls, and most pairs can now raise only one brood each year instead of two. Many birds, forced from their former haunts, found rich new hunting grounds along roadside verges and motorway reservations, only to be dazzled by headlights and killed by traffic. Others have been drawn to railway embankments for the same reasons, and then hit by trains. At the same time, the old barns and outbuildings in which owls have nested for hundreds of years have been going as fast as the birds themselves. Some have simply fallen down, like the beautiful tithe barn in Powerstock itself, whose thatched roof was too costly to repair. Others have been replaced by inhospitable modern buildings with no room for owls. And out in the hedgerows the loss of more than 22 million elm trees, wiped out by Dutch elm disease, has dealt the barn owl another blow. For, despite its name, four out of every ten pairs nest in hollow trees.

The future looks bleak, but there is hope. A local barn owl rescue group has been formed, and is persuading local farmers to adopt pairs of aviary-bred birds in the hope that their offspring can be returned to the wild. So maybe the bird I saw tonight will survive long enough to find a mate and stay to breed. One pair used to nest regularly in a disused, ivy-covered limekiln in the next valley, but even they have disappeared. It would be nice to think of a new pair taking over. The young owlets are less than appealing: drab, woolly bundles the colour of an unwashed vest, with vulturine heads and a rank smell. But adulthood transforms them into creatures of unearthly beauty, and I hope we shall see them again from the cottage as we used to, on midsummer evenings, wavering over the meadow grasses on thistle-down wings.

Barn owl

DECEMBER

10 December
Slimbridge, Gloucestershire

Curlews were stalking over the roadside fields as I crossed the Sharpness-to-Gloucester canal. Their hunched brown shapes were everywhere, probing with long, curved bills for worms. These level pasturelands in the Berkeley Vale have a long tradition of good husbandry. This is the English Normandy – renowned for cider and cream and Double Gloucester cheese. For centuries its fame centred around Berkeley Castle, the oldest inhabited stronghold in England, built in 1153 and still lived in by the Berkeley family. In summer, tourists flock there to admire the castle treasures and peer into the dismal cell where, in 1327, Edward II was put to death in so foul a manner that his screams, it is said, could be heard a mile away in Berkeley village.

But in winter the greatest attraction for miles around is the Wildfowl Trust at Slimbridge. Of all the seasonal movements of wildlife which sweep the British countryside there is nothing to match the great migrations of wintering wildfowl, and nowhere better to thrill to the sight and sound of Bewick's swans, wigeon and thousands of noisy white-fronted geese than the hides and viewing towers of Slimbridge.

The Trust is a non-profit-making organization established in 1946 by Sir Peter Scott. He started with just 17 acres on the New Grounds, a three-mile stretch of high saltmarsh and enclosed pastureland reclaimed from the Severn estuary in the 1600s. For centuries the area and its adjoining tidal flats had been a traditional wintering ground for geese, maintained for sport by the Berkeley family. Now the Trust owns 100 acres of enclosed ponds, pens and hides, and controls a further 1200 acres as a wildfowl refuge. During the summer, sheep and cattle graze the refuge; but from October onwards they are withdrawn

OPPOSITE: *Valley of the West Dart near Wistman's Wood, Dartmoor, Devon*

OVERLEAF: *Bewick's swans, Slimbridge, Gloucestershire*

61

primaries
hidden.

gliding

turbulence
down back
of neck

Noisey
approach!
(braking
sharply)

taking off.

almost.
parallel

from the fields, leaving the grass for geese and wigeon.

I arrived to the clamour of Canada geese, members of a feral flock which breed on the gravel pits at Frampton, two miles upriver. Now they flew noisily overhead to join the duck and Bewick's swans assembled on the waters of the Rushy Pen, anticipating the free handouts of grain. A notice outside the Halfway Hide announced yesterday's tally for visiting birdwatchers: 4000 wigeon, 1800 white-fronted geese, 224 Bewick's swans, 350 pochard, 2 bean geese and single sightings of pink-footed goose, peregrine, little owl, snipe and water rail. These numbers, although impressive, were still only a fraction of all the birds to be seen. Up to 40,000 common and black-headed gulls roost on the mudflats. Clouds of starlings swirl over the saltmarsh, feeding in company with hundreds of lapwings, curlew, dunlin, redwing and fieldfare; and over the next few weeks, as the weather turned colder, the northeast winds would bring even more wildfowl pouring down from the Arctic, until the skies over Slimbridge become a maelstrom of circling flocks.

Beyond the slit windows of Halfway Hide, wigeon were mustered in dense congregations on the wide meadow called the Tack Piece. They are the most numerous of all the duck at Slimbridge, followed by mallard, pintail, shoveler, tufted duck, teal and pochard. The wigeon come from Iceland and Siberia, building up to a peak of around 5000 birds in January. They are beautiful creatures, especially the drakes with their cinnamon heads and delicate, close-grained winter plumage, and I love to hear their whistled exclamations as they come flighting in through the murk of a December dusk. Now they were feeding peacefully in cold, bright sunlight, packed so close together that the flock seemed to flow over the grass in a feathered tide of bobbing heads.

Where shallow flashes reflected the sky, teal swam among spikes of rushes. Others joined them, coming in fast and low like waders, disturbing a water rail which slunk deeper into cover. On the far side of the field a little owl sat on a fence post under bare trees. Nearby, a family group of four Bewick's swans were grazing; and all the time the sky was filled with the constant movement of birds: languid gulls, fast-flying pintail, echelons of swans and yodelling packs of white-fronted geese.

The white-fronts – so-called because the pink bill is set off by a white mask which stops just in front of the eyes – are by far the commonest species at Slimbridge. The first groups arrive in October, having completed an epic journey of more than 2000 miles from their breeding grounds in Arctic Russia. Towards Christmas their numbers build up until the flocks are 7000 strong. They are noisy birds, constantly calling

White-fronted goose

with shrill, chuckling voices. Powerful fliers, they are the most agile of all the grey geese, able to turn swiftly and slide away down the sky. A skein came in now, bunching and swirling as they spilled the wind from their wings to drop steeply into the field. The watchers in the hide fell silent. Nowhere else in Britain do the wary white-fronts come so close.

Afterwards I moved on to the Holden Tower, a two-storey wooden hide facing the Severn across the great saltmarsh known as the Dumbles. The estuary here is about a mile wide and subject to fierce, racing tides which raise the level of the river by some 33 feet, drowning the mudflats and driving the birds off the saltings; but now the tide was out. It was cold in the hide. A north wind cut like a knife through the narrow windows as I watched a female peregrine glide past, setting off a frenzy of starlings in her wake. She turned and rose above the loitering river. Her sharp wings drove her swiftly back towards the tower, and I could see her huge, luminous eyes burning as she flicked past; then she turned away once more, lifted over the sea wall and settled far out on the Dumbles, where she began to bathe.

Drake pintail

Slowly the panic subsided. The wheeling flocks put up by the falcon fell back to earth in languorous spirals and began to feed again, fanning out over the grass. The day was drawing to a close. Sunk between its tidal flats, the Severn lay sullen. On the far bank, beyond the silhouette of Awre church, the land rose and rolled away to the Forest of Dean, soft with distance. The sun was going. Willows glinted in its last rays, flaring red across the fields, but there remained one last excitement. Out of the sky, faint at first but growing louder, rang a wild music, more fitting for a Russian forest than a Gloucestershire river valley, as a flock of Bewick's swans came in from the fields where they had been grazing.

Their presence at Slimbridge is a tribute to the work of Sir Peter Scott and the Wildfowl Trust. The first Bewick's ever to be recorded on the Severn estuary was almost certainly decoyed from its traditional wintering grounds on the Somerset Levels by the presence of some tame North American whistling swans. That was in 1948. Since then, numbers have steadily increased until more than 300 swans now winter at Slimbridge for weeks on end. Like the white-fronts, they come from the tundra of Arctic Russia, and are part of the 5500-strong population which regularly overwinters in the British Isles. Some have been coming to Slimbridge for more than twenty years, and every bird can be individually recognized by its unique black and yellow bill pattern, in the same way that human beings can be distinguished by their fingerprints.

They flew now in the dying light, white as snowflakes in a blue haze of dusk downpouring, coming together in long, wavering streamers. For a moment there was silence. Their beating wings gave out no sound – so different from the mute swans' singing pinions. Then again I heard the exultant chorus, falling, fading as the birds bore away to settle on Swan Lake. There they would roost secure in the foxproof pen, huddling for warmth on three small islands until dawn.

14 December

Powerstock, Dorset

Today I heard the strangest story. Dennis, who lives in the hamlet across the valley and who sometimes gives me an early-morning lift into Dorchester, has lived in the country all his life. He knows the ways of birds and animals, and I have no reason to doubt his word. One day last week he left home as usual at 7 a.m., and it was still dark when he set off through the narrow lanes. As he drove up the steep hill which leads to the top of Eggardon, a huge fallow buck pushed its way through the hedge and stopped in the road in front of him.

Dennis pulled in to the side of the lane and revved the engine, but the buck stood its ground. Very quietly, Dennis opened the car door and got out. The buck shook its broad antlers but did not run. Its behaviour was extraordinary. Afterwards, Dennis said that he had felt hypnotized – frightened in case the buck might charge him, yet at the same time compelled to continue. Slowly he took a step forward, and then another; and still the buck did not move. Then, as if in a dream, he was reaching out and stroking the animal's muzzle. For a moment – he could not say how long – they stood together in the headlights' glare. Then, suddenly, as if it had caught a sound which Dennis could not hear, the buck turned and trotted off up the lane into the darkness.

17–18 December

Dartmoor, Devon

The moor has always been a place apart. Raised above the rest of Devon, it is the last great wilderness in southern Britain, aloof and withdrawn – high country where the sky feels closer and it is possible to walk in winter for miles over bare brown hills and seldom meet a soul. Dartmoor is haunted, bittersweet and poignant; one minute an aching emptiness of peat hag and heather, the next a deep valley at your feet, a falling away of mossy oaks, the sudden gleam of a salmon river. But above all it is granite country, stern and rainswept; a world of cleaves, clitters, tors and quakers – Dartmoor words for glens, screes, inselbergs and oozing bogs. Its hillsides are littered with relics of forgotten people. Bronze Age circles and grizzled monoliths stand marooned in seas of dying bracken.

The oldest living thing on Dartmoor is Wistman's Wood. On the Ordnance Survey map it is simply a small, green teardrop in the valley of the West Dart above Two Bridges; but trees of any kind are rare on the high moor, and a broad-leaved wood at 1400 feet is almost a miracle.

The day had started bright and benign – at Drewsteignton it had been almost warm enough to sit outside in the village square – but it did not last. On the high moor the sun vanished and a cold wind blew. Cloud thickened. All colour drained from the landscape. In the valley below, riders were moving in single file. Their scarlet coats shone like sparks against the dun slopes, and the sound of a hunting horn drifted up on the wind, thin and insistent, calling to hounds as they sought a fox in the furze under Merripit Hill.

The path from Two Bridges was easy to follow. Blobs of yellow paint splashed on rocks marked the way across the fields. At the head of the valley Crow Tor glowered on the skyline, guarding the West Dart's boggy birthplace. A mile and a half after leaving the road, I entered the wood.

Moss, fern and lichen

The most remarkable feature of Wistman's Wood is its lack of height. It is composed almost entirely of ancient pedunculate oaks, so gnarled and stunted that few exceed 15 feet. It is a troll wood, sinister and storm-stricken, a pagan grove whose close-knit canopy conceals a tumbling chaos of mossy boulders and slabs of moorstone as big as grand pianos. Woodrush and polypody ferns thrive everywhere in its damp gloom; and every tree, each dwarfish trunk and wizened limb, is lagged with lichen, thick as sheep's wood. In woodland terms it is a living monument as precious as any parish church; and if Chiltern beechwoods can be likened to Gothic cathedrals, then Wistman's Wood is a Dark Age undercroft.

By any reckoning it is one of the seven wonders of the moor, and many writers have been drawn to it. The earliest description is by Tristram Risdon, writing in 1620, who named it as one of Dartmoor's three most memorable sights; but its pedigree is much older. Cross-ing's *Guide to Dartmoor* suggests two possible earlier versions of its

OVERLEAF: *Wistman's Wood, Dartmoor, Devon*

67

Otter

name, both of which would suggest a history of at least a thousand years. One, *Uisg maen coed*, is Celtic and means the Stony Wood by the Water. The other, Wealasman's Wood, is Saxon, but means the Wood of the Celts; and in living memory there were still moorfolk who called it Welshman's Wood.

Until this century the wood was so dense and low-growing that it was almost impenetrable, inhabited only by foxes who made their lairs beneath its rocks. There hounds could not follow and huntsmen could not dislodge them even with crowbars and terriers. Since then, grazing and greater public access to the moor have opened it up to such an extent that the Nature Conservancy Council, which manages the wood as a nature reserve, is concerned for its future. Like so many natural features of the countryside it is unwittingly being damaged by innocent visitors who come here only to walk, and in time unrestricted access may no longer be possible. Already the NCC has fenced off an experimental plot to monitor the changes which occur when grazing animals and trampling humans are excluded.

Inside the wood, no birds sang. The acid colours of the mosses shone out in sharp counterpoint to the dead bracken and fallen leaves piled up in the hollows between the rocks. Rotted by winter rain, they would provide rich humus for the new year's flowers: wood sorrel, foxglove, herb robert and tormentil. I did not go deep into the wood. The words of the NCC rang in my ears: 'The vegetation is fragile and deteriorating; please help us to protect it.' Instead I sat on a mossy moorstone slab beneath the twisted trees and listened to the infant River Dart hissing down the valley, and thought it one of the most hallowed places in Britain.

I had walked up the valley dryshod. Now, true to its fickle nature, Dartmoor had turned hostile, and the northeast wind drove a drenching rain across the stony fields. Caught in the open, I had no alternative but to push on to Two Bridges. The hotel bar was deserted but a fire of massive ash logs warmed the room. I ordered a bowl of chicken broth and a hot pasty, and sat beneath the grinning mask of an 18½ lb dog otter, killed on the Plym in 1932 – the year that Henry Williamson's country classic, *Tarka the Otter* was published.

Outside, rain had given way to hail which beat a furious tattoo on the road. At Princetown the grim old prison, built in 1806 to accommodate French prisoners of war, seemed even more forbidding under lashing hail. Beyond Hessary Tor a stony track led to Foggin Tor quarries. When the hailstorm had passed over I went to the deserted workings to look for ravens, but the only signs of life were the ubiquitous Dartmoor sheep, which seemed impervious to the cold.

Wherever the turf had been closely nibbled, the hail lay where it fell and did not melt; so that when at last the sun returned, slanting through black reefs of cloud, the hillsides shimmered in fresh coats of rime. To the south I could see the bunched and burnished coils of the Tamar, and the Cornish sea beyond; and, to the west, all the hills of Cornwall and fresh squalls approaching. It was time to go. I returned to the car and drove over the moors to Cator Court, a thatched stone farmstead near Widecombe.

Cator Court is the home of Dartmoor's most redoubtable guardian, Sylvia, Lady Sayer, and her husband, Admiral Sir Guy Sayer. For many years, as the driving force behind the Dartmoor Preservation Association, she had been a thorn in the sides of farmers, water boards, local authorities and all those who simply regarded Dartmoor as a profitless wasteland. She fought and won the battle to save the wild heartland of the southern moor from the proposed Swincombe reservoir, but lost the fight to prevent the drowning of the Meldon Valley. Today, despite advancing age and the loss of an eye, she is as indomitable as ever. 'After all,' she said with a mischievous twinkle, 'didn't Nelson win all his greatest victories with only one eye?'

A true Dartmoor dwelling, Cator Court is built of granite with flagstone floors, a circular stone staircase and a great open hearth surmounted by a single massive block of moorstone, and has been standing for at least five hundred years. The original homestead was even older. It was founded by Cada, a Saxon and probably a thegn of Earl Harold, who held much land in the region. As long-time residents of Cator, the Sayers are entitled to commoners' rights, including that of turbary, which allows them to cut turf on the moor. On Dartmoor these ancient privileges are known as Venville Rights, a term derived from the Latin, *fines villarum*, and are jealously preserved. They go back to the fourteenth century, when Richard II gave custody of the Forest of Dartmoor to Richard de Abberbury, and it was agreed that all moormen should be allowed to take turf, heather, furze and stone from the hills, and to graze their beasts. Only two things were forbidden to them: green oak and red venison.

The turf is cut in blocks known as vags, with a tool known as a vagging iron, and is taken from a trench called a turf-tie. After the vags have been dug out, the owner must replace the top turf to maintain the sward in unscarred condition. The vags are dug in summer and then stacked to dry for use as winter fuel; when the peat is burnt it fills the houses with its ancient fragrance.

On either side of the Cator fireplace hung two black iron clappers with a curious history. Once they rang the bells of Widecombe, and swung in the high, pinnacled tower of the parish church, pride of the tin miners through whose wealth it was raised. But in 1638, in the midst of a Sunday service, a sudden storm struck the church, destroying a pinnacle, killing four worshippers and injuring more than sixty others. Afterwards, survivors recalled seeing a mysterious stranger with a cloven foot. Thus was the Devil's visit to Widecombe added to the myths and superstitions that cling to Dartmoor like hanging mist. And later, when the tower was repaired and the bells restored, the old clappers lay forgotten until they were rediscovered and bought for a few shillings by Sylvia Sayer's mother.

Outside, in the dark, the wind moaned around the old house; but inside it was snug and warm. In hard winters the Sayers are cut off less often now that tractors and bulldozers can clear the drifts from sunken lanes; but Dartmoor is notorious for severe weather. The worst winter in living memory was in 1893. That was the year of the Great Blizzard, which began on 9 March and raged for thirty-six hours, cutting off Cornwall from the rest of the country and marooning parts of the moor for a month. So fierce was the cold that snow lay upon the high moor until well into May. It is at times such as these, when a rapid thaw after heavy snow is halted by a sudden sharp drop in temperature, or where rain freezes where it has fallen, that the moorland phenomenon known as the ammil may occur. Then, when dawn comes, every blade of grass, every fence post and wind-blasted thorn is locked inside its own icicle. Fronds of bracken become filigree jewels. The entire moor shivers and sparkles with frost fire. Even the granite tors glitter like black glaciers. It is a spectacle of unearthly arctic beauty, but it also brings great suffering for the creatures of the moor – sheep, wild ponies, birds and rabbits – for whom there is no shelter in such savage cold. The last great ammil (the name comes from the Old English *ammal*, meaning enamel) was in 1947, and took a heavy toll of Dartmoor ponies.

Next morning, rain beat against the windows and the hills were hidden in sagging cloud. With a force nine gale imminent I resisted the temptation to visit Jackman's Bottom, a boggy hole near the lonely summit of Great Kneeset, in the remote and sodden heart of the northern moor. When visibility is bad it is all too easy to lose one's way in the waterlogged hills and spend most of the day picking a way round the sphagnum-covered mires known as 'Dartmoor stables' because so many ponies have foundered in their quaking depths. Even in the shelter of the valleys there was little pleasure in walking. The rain cascaded down the narrow lanes, and the trees thrashed before the wind. Retreat seemed honourable, and good fortune was at hand.

'Keep heart – you're still en route,' said the signpost in the back lanes beyond Chagford. The sign had been erected by the owners of the Gidleigh Park Hotel, so remote and hard to find is this welcome oasis of warmth and comfort on the upper reaches of the North Teign River. For the past seven years Gidleigh Park has been run by an American couple, Paul and Kay Henderson. In that time they have collected an enviable list of gastronomic stars and rosettes, and have transformed their elegant mock-Tudor mansion into the finest country house hotel I know. Log fires burn day and night. There are only twelve rooms, each one a spacious retreat furnished with comfortable armchairs and offering far-reaching views across the Teign Valley. Gidleigh Park is expensive. But on a bleak winter's day, tired and cold and soaked to the skin, there were few other luxuries I would have exchanged for its hot bath, marvellous dinner and a bottle of Paul Henderson's best white burgundy.

22 December
Powerstock, Dorset

Days of torrential rain had left the countryside awash. Travelling home to Dorset by train from London, I looked out on a desolation of sodden fields and streaming ditches. Today was the winter solstice, the shortest day. Under lowering skies the old year was not so much laid to rest as swept away in torrents of rain.

As the train raced across the New Forest, the rain began again. Dark conifers massed on distant horizons. All the bogs and bottoms were brimming. I saw no deer; only scattered groups of shaggy ponies, heads down and facing the wind with stoic indifference.

Everywhere, rivers ran swollen and heavy with silt. At South-ampton the Itchen had burst its banks and spilled across the relic watermeadows, attracting herons and redshanks which flew up in alarm as the train rushed past. At Poole the tide was up, and rafts of shelduck bobbed on the grey wavelets between the railway line and the shores of the Arne peninsula. Sullen cloud hung over the Purbecks, obscuring the gap where the ruin of Corfe Castle leers like a rotten molar. Beyond Wareham the Frome had flooded, as it does every winter, transforming Hardy's 'Vale of the Little Dairies' into a watery fen of half-drowned willows and disconsolate cattle.

And so to Dorchester, the dour grey town brightened by Christmas lights, and out along the Roman road beyond, past Maiden Castle and

73

over the downs to Eggardon, and the final plunge through the hollow lanes of dear, damp Dorset. I was home for Christmas.

23 December

Powerstock, Dorset

The log man called this morning, so at least we should be warm this Christmas. Better than roses, better than bread fresh from the oven, better even than breakfast coffee and bacon frying is the smell of a good log fire. Never mind the hard labour, the smuts and ashes, the howling draughts and the sheer inefficiency of a form of heating which flings most of its warmth up the chimney. The homely reek of wood smoke carries with it the ache of nostalgia. Even in today's centrally heated and double-glazed winters, the sight and smell of an open fire kindles an atavistic pleasure which goes back far beyond the roaring inglenooks of Dickensian coaching inns. And at Christmas, traditionally a time for the burning of yule logs, a wood fire seems to give out more than just a physical glow.

Sadly, the art of logmanship has been largely forgotten. For, just like wines, there are good logs and bad logs. Some spit like angry leopards, while others burn as serenely as church candles. Oak is hard to beat if it is old and dry enough, burning slowly with a fierce, red glow, though its smell has an acrid edge which can catch the throat. Beech is another generous burner, but again it needs to be dry and well seasoned. The same goes for elm, long underrated but of late the most abundant of fuels as a result of the Dutch elm plague. Silver birch guarantees a fiery pyromaniac display, but burns too fast. All the pines are lively and make excellent kindling, especially larch twigs. But while conifers give out a fine, aromatic smell – and none more so than cedar – they also spit and crackle like small arms fire. Apple, pear and cherry logs are much sought after for their fragrance. Holly makes good, solid logs which will burn green and still give off a bright, clean flame. Hawthorn is another heavy wood which, like holly, burns well even when green and produces a tremendous amount of heat. Chestnut, willow and poplar come well down the list, and alder last of all. But the finest fuel in the forest is undoubtedly the ash. Here, truly, is a wood to warm you twice: once in the sawing and again in the burning. The dry twigs which the tree casts off in winter gales are ideal for kindling. The sawn faggots can be burnt as green as the day the sap rose in them, and a grate piled with seasoned ash logs is indeed a fire to come home to.

In the afternoon, armed with a pair of secateurs, I set out on a last-minute search for holly to decorate the cottage. Holly is a common tree in west Dorset. In Powerstock parish, and north as far as Corscombe, and westward right across the Marshwood Vale to Fishpond Bottom, the lanes and hedgerows have kept their holly even when other trees have been felled or pulverized by mechanical flails. I have heard it said locally that it is unlucky to cut down a holly; so maybe supersition has succeeded where the Wildlife and Countryside Act has failed. A month ago I had earmarked several trees whose branches were bowed with the weight of glossy berries. The autumn was exceptionally fruitful and they had ripened early. Now, to my dismay, there was not a berry to be seen. All had been stripped by birds. Only the old churchyard hollies still held their Christmas bounty, glowing among the shiny leaves. Why the birds should have left these trees untouched is a mystery. A neighbour suggested that the birds associate them with the berries of churchyard yews. Or maybe the blackbirds and wintering fieldfares and redwings prefer the hollies of the open country and shun the village churchyards except in times of severe weather?

It was tempting to take a modest sprig or two, so thickly were the berries clustered on the bowed branches beside the lych gate. But to

rob a churchyard of its holly seemed like an act of desecration. Instead, I remembered one last chance of success before dark – a solitary tree that grew beside one of the high lanes on the way to Toller. In the swiftly falling dusk the tree loomed so darkly that I could not make out any scarlet spots among the leaves until I was almost underneath it. The berries were few, and others had been there before me. But there was enough for a sprig for the pudding and one for the house. Once again the old tree had not let me down. Gratefully I clipped off my modest requirements and drove home. Christmas would have seemed incomplete without holly.

25 December

Powerstock, Dorset

Christmas Day in Dorset is often mild. My daughter longed for snow, but today was the mildest December weather I could remember. By midday the thermometer in the garden was registering 55°F in the shade, and just as well. I had planned to chop a fresh supply of kindling yesterday, go for a walk, astonish the regular churchgoers by turning up for the Christmas Eve carol service, and maybe call at the pub to check the results of the Christmas raffle. Instead I awoke with a heavy cold and so did none of those things, but nursed a medicinal tot of Greek brandy and went to bed early.

But that is jumping the gun. Although I had spent yesterday morning huddled by the fireside, I felt well enough in the afternoon to assist with the preparations for the Christmas lunch, the highlight of which was a plump 12 lb goose. For weeks it had been fattening with its companions on a farm lower down the valley. We had often seen them as we drove into Bridport: a white flock grazing on the green hills of West Milton. A week ago they had gone to market. Now the corpse hung cold in the porch, stripped of its feathers except for a few obstinate quills. At times such as this I think seriously of vegetarianism, but I am too old for redemption. So down came the goose from its peg in the porch – and off with its head! We took the skin from the neck, sewed up one end and stuffed it with sausagemeat for supper, to be served with red cabbage and baked jacket potatoes. Then we stuffed the bird itself, using a splendid West Country recipe which called for chopped apples soaked in rum, celery, chopped goose liver, breadcrumbs, seasoning and a pinch of nutmeg, all bound together with an egg.

Now Christmas Day had come, and it was so warm that we did not bother to light the room stove. Besides, the kitchen was warm enough as the goose had been sizzling in the oven since 9 a.m. Already its appetizing smell had begun to permeate the house, as the recipe insisted on regular bastings with warm cider. A few morning chores still remained to be done: down to the garden to pick the sprouts and bring back the big red Désirée potatoes that grow so well in our light soil. Lifted in late summer, they are stored in a chest in the shed and are good to eat until mid-February. I made a mental note to net the remaining sprouts and purple sprouting broccoli before the pigeons could massacre them. Nearby, where I had rolled back a carpet of weeds and forked over the black earth, our resident robin searched for worms.

Our kitchen garden is separated from the cottage, and lies on the Knap some 50 yards away: half an acre of Dorset hillside rented for a nominal sum to keep us supplied with home-grown fruit and vegetables. Self-sufficiency was never our aim; but at least we are no longer totally dependent on the whims of fluctuating Euromarts. It's an odd piece of ground, like a double-decker slice of disused vineyard, drunkenly tilting as if about to lurch into the lane below. Once it was a lynchet, a medieval strip field. Perhaps it is of the same age as King Athelstan's castle on the other side of the valley. Certainly the Saxons had an eye for good land: our plot basks on a south-facing slope with a wall at its back, well drained and shielded from the prevailing south-westerlies by the flank of the hill. In the Middle Ages flax might have grown there, blue as a summer sky, to be cropped, retted, scutched and hackled to provide yarn and sailcloth for West Country seamen.

Twenty years ago it had become a well-tended vegetable plot, diligently hoed, with onion beds and runner beans and a patch where

free-range hens took dust baths in the sun. Eventually it proved too much for the old cottager who kept it, and the land fell fallow. In the space of a decade, nature took over. Where carrots and onions had fattened in orderly rows, brambles rolled in barbed wire tangles over infestations of nettles and rampant couch-grass. That was how it was when we arrived, like fugitives from the Monmouth Rebellion, armed with bramble scythes and long-handled slashers to reclaim the wilderness. When the brambles were vanquished and put to the torch there still remained the shock-headed clumps of couch to be cleared, sinewy hawsers of old man's beard, and nettle roots, gnarled and yellow, so stubbornly anchored in the earth that it took a mattock to prise them loose.

Now, looking back, it is hard to recognize that overgrown jungle in the wall-to-wall carpets of finely raked tilth, rich and deep like fine-ground coffee, and the burgeoning rows of sprouts and broccoli. Can this trim kitchen garden with its strawberry beds and fruit trees be the same unkempt battlefield where we burned the vengeful brambles and slew the nettlebeds ten years ago?

By now the day was like early spring. Outside the cottage the arching stems of winter jasmine were a mass of yellow stars, and on the south-facing bank of the lane that descends to Eastwater Farm, among new green shoots of nettles and cow parsley, wild violets were in bloom. Bravest of flowers, they are always the first to appear around the turn of the year. And one more treasure: in Castle Mill Lane, where hart's tongue ferns and ash tree roots bind crumbling banks of fox-mould earth, a primrose clump had put out no fewer than eight pale flowers. Here was yet another sign that even now, in the very depths of winter, new life was stirring. Everywhere in the surrounding hedgerows the ash buds were swelling and gangs of long-tailed tits swung in the fattening hazel catkins.

We sat down to eat at one o'clock. The goose filled the kitchen with hot fat smells as the close-grained meat fell away under the knife in perfect slices, each one encircled by a crisp brown rim of skin. Roast potatoes, sprouts, spoonsful of stuffing and rich gravy accompanied it, and a wonderful bottle of Chardonnay wine, light and mellow, with a delicate aftertaste of vanilla bequeathed by the cask of Limousin oak in which it had matured. Last, the Christmas pudding, decorated with its sprig of holly, was borne in triumph to the table, trailing its own dark brown aroma.

Wine and warmth did their work. When drowsiness came we did not resist it but put a match to the fire and fell asleep by its blaze. Later, when it had grown dark outside, we drew the curtains and watched the firelight winking like frost in the tinsel on the Christmas tree. My daughter lit a candle, and its pure flame cast wavering shadows on the walls, adding to that indefinable sense of mystery and contentment which Christmas always brings, and which has never lost its magic for me, but remains as poignant as childhood lost. The house lay quiet. The red logs hissed in the hearth, the two cats curled up in its warmth. Everything was as it should be: a family together and peace on earth – at least in this small corner of it.

26 December
Powerstock, Dorset

Red fox

Boxing Day, and Dorset was as sodden as an unsqueezed sponge. There was no wind to disperse the quick, sharp taint of fox in the lane; a grand day for the hunt, but a bad one for the hunted. The ash on the hill was black with rooks. They stared expectantly from the bare branches like an undertakers' convention waiting for a corpse to bury.

For the first time I heard the horn, faint and far off. From the crest of the knoll I looked for movement in the rolling spread of fields below. There they were: a distant glimpse of brindled hounds, plunging like porpoises in a sea of kale, and a whipper-in, one solitary scarlet spark against a sombre coppice.

Suddenly there was a crash of sound and the baying of hounds grew deeper, more menacing. Hidden by the hill, the music came closer. I waited in the hedge for the entry of the fugitive. He appeared within minutes: a big dog fox, going flat out across the ploughland, his winter coat the colour of dead bracken, his long tail fluffed out behind. He didn't run; he flowed through the furrows, three fields ahead of the pack.

Flying in his wake came the hounds, crying on a sure line as they burst through the first hedge in a tan and cream chevron. As yet there was no sign of the huntsmen, but the fox's lead was already cut to two fields and shrinking fast as he dropped into Combe Bottom. Then there was confusion: milling hounds, stampeding sheep, startled rooks swirling overhead. The hunt was foxed.

How had it happened? Maybe it is wrong to read cunning into animal behaviour. To suggest that the fox had deliberately planned this diversion would be to credit him with powers he cannot possess. But his tactics were faultless. A quick twist and he was doubling back up the combe while the pack were still casting around to pick up his line

Hoar frost

again, and the first riders arrived, red-faced and breathless on mud-spattered horses.

By now other onlookers had gathered. Nearby stood a father with three sons. We were the only ones to have seen the fox reappear. 'You won't tell, will you?' said one of the boys anxiously. Together we watched the fox race through a cottage garden among rows of Brussels sprouts stripped for Christmas dinner, into a farmyard where his scent would be smothered by richer smells, and away to the sanctuary of Knoll Wood.

Why does foxhunting cause such bitter controversy? Is it really just a question of blood and cruelty on the one side, sport and tradition on the other? Or do the old antagonisms go deeper? There are those who would argue that the hunt is a ritual: a reaffirmation of the power of the gentry, a rubbing of Norman salt into Saxon wounds which nine hundred years have failed to heal.

My own views are hopelessly ambivalent. To watch a hunt streaming across a watercolour landscape of furrow, combe and spinney is to know the quintessence of the countryside in winter: all England distilled into one classic sporting print. I accept, too, that foxes must be culled; that in the absence of other predators in our half-tame countryside, man must keep the balance, and would do so more ruthlessly if huntsmen themselves did not have a vested interest in the perpetuation of their quarry. Yet I cannot deny the relief I felt when I watched that fox go free.

30 December
Powerstock, Dorset

It is always now, in the hungover aftermath of the Christmas holiday, that winter seems to bite harder. Hoar frost lingers all day under the hedges and the ground is iron underfoot. But it was not the cold that urged us over the fields at forced march tempo. Our walk had the purpose and precision of a military exercise. Fuel for free was our objective: the need to top up our dwindling log stack with dead wood.

Today we went to the wood where the fallow deer lived. There I knew the pickings would be easy. The forest floor is a charnel house of dead limbs shaken loose from geriatric oaks by the gales that come blustering up the valley from Lyme Bay. A modest-sized power station could no doubt consume the entire wood in a week, but there is more than enough to keep us going.

No ordinary wood, this. Wild and wolfish in the winter light, it pours across the head of the combe in a writhing tide of tangled boughs, dank and lichen-bearded. It is of the same wizened pedigree as Wistman's Wood on Dartmoor; and its goblin oaks exude the same vague air of disquiet. Why should the silence under those misshapen candelabras appear so sinister? It is a forest fey enough for Merlin. Above looms the dark presence of Eggardon, where motorists coming by night over the Roman road are still afraid to look in the mirror lest they glimpse the ghost of a woman who has been known to appear, unbidden, in the back seat.

The wood is a remnant, a relic of the old primeval oakwood that once covered most of Britain. It was here in King Athelstan's reign, before the Norman Conquest. (There is still a King's Farm at the edge of the forest.) It was here long before the Romans trod their road over the downs from Dorchester. It is as old as the Stone Age, one of those rare and diminishing scraps of the land surface where man has made little impact.

Ours has been an age of unprecedented woodland destruction. All over Britain, from Dorset to the Highlands, the woods are falling fast. In the past thirty years we have lost half our ancient semi-natural woodlands, and still the devastation continues. But what are 'ancient' woods, and why should we preserve them? The Nature Conservancy Council's definition is a site which has been wooded since at least 1600. Some of these old woods may have originated in the Dark Ages, and studies by historical ecologists such as Dr Oliver Rackham show that some are older still. They may well be direct descendants of what he calls the wildwood – the primeval forest which covered Britain after the last Ice Age.

Dr Rackham's findings have given fresh impetus to the campaign to identify and preserve these most ancient links with our past at a time when commercial interests regard them as the derelict junkyards of a forgotten industry. Now there is a new awareness that old woods have a value beyond the balance sheet. At last they are being recognized for what they are: living records of our environment, deeply rooted in the lives and affections of local people, to be cherished in much the same way as the parish church.

Ancient woodland is also a natural oasis, host to a rich community of plants and animals which are the direct descendants of Britain's primeval wildlife. That is why their value in conservation terms is beyond price. Once destroyed, such woodland can never be re-created; and the species it harbours cannot easily survive outside its protective canopy. Right up until the twentieth century, the wildlife that relied on ancient woods – lichens, fungi, birds, mammals, butterflies of the woodland rides, shade-loving plants – all survived in a deep peace. True woodland denizens are expert at marking time: the rare military orchid, now confined to a couple of Chiltern glades, may bloom only once in twenty years; but no plant can withstand the bulldozer and the plough.

In the beginning was the wildwood, home of the wolf and the brown bear. Six thousand years ago it covered most of the country. Even the summits of the Pennines lay buried in its leafy silence. Five thousand years earlier, Britain's primeval forests had begun to take root on the open tundra left by the retreating glaciers. The melting of the ice had not yet formed the English Channel, and waves of colonizing trees spread north and west from the Continent. First came juniper; then birch and pine, followed by a succession of familiar broad-leaved trees: hazel, elm, oak and alder. Later came the small-leaved lime, the last invader to cross the land-bridge before Britain became an island.

When the Stone Age dawned, most of Britain was virgin forest, a temperate jungle whose ancestry may still be recognized in today's ancient woods. But by now the first inroads had begun to appear in the once endless canopy. Pollen counts from the prehistoric peat, which record a sudden decline of elm around 3000 BC, also show a corresponding increase in nettles and other farm weeds. The dismantling of the wildwood by Neolithic farmers had begun.

When the Celtic tribes arrived with their iron tools and heavy ploughs the rate of attrition was greater still. With axe, fire and browsing beasts they laid bare millions of acres. The Romans continued the process, converting much of lowland Britain into an imperial granary; yet in ninth-century Saxon England large tracts of natural forest still remained. The Kent and Sussex Weald stretched for 120 miles. North of the Thames another great forest extended from the Chilterns to the Essex marshes. In the Midlands the vanished Bruneswald covered much of Huntingdonshire and Northamptonshire. Further north lay Sherwood. In Scotland stood the great wood of Caledon. And in Dorset, under the steep slopes of Eggardon, the crooked oaks rose and fell in an endless cycle of decay and rebirth.

By the time of the Norman Conquest, the open pattern of our modern countryside was well established. The Saxons had already fixed the boundaries of woods, fields and parishes in patterns still recognizable today. By the Middle Ages woods had become valuable properties, privately owned, diligently embanked and surrounded by a fence or hedge to keep out grazing animals. Medieval Britain was a woodland economy. It was an age when men learned to live with their woods, to manage them as a self-renewing resource instead of clear-felling them as if trees were barley.

The decline, when it came, was not due to the Tudor ironmasters and charcoal burners. Nor was it caused by the shipwrights who built the Georgian battle fleets. Then, as now, it was agriculture that forced the woods to retreat. Railways and the age of cheap coal undercut the firewood trade. The coppice woodlands of the Home Counties which had once warmed London fell derelict. Two world wars, the felling of timber to pay death duties and the scourge of Dutch elm disease carried off much of what remained, and the easy profits and tax benefits of replacing slow-growing hardwoods with quick cash crops of conifers have done the rest.

Today Britain, after Ireland, is the most naked country in Europe. The old wildwood is gone for ever, but what remains is even more precious: a scattered mosaic of clumps and coppices, silent spinneys, lonely fox roosts, beech hangers, Wealden shaws, pagan groves of oak and holly; and sometimes, among the bare trunks, the dark shadows receding, the echo of a true forest.

Such was the wood we had entered today. The frost had not penetrated its boggy bottoms, and the ground squelched underfoot, threatening to suck the boots from our feet. Winding between tall clumps of pendulous sedge, we left a trail of muddy footprints, each one slowly filling with water. Ours were not the only tracks. Incised in black humus and yellow clay were the cloven slots of fallow deer, for whom the wood is a refuge from poachers.

When the light began to fail we retraced our steps. In the wood's hollow heart, with no landmarks to steer by, it is all too easy to lose one's way. Dusk seeped like silt between the trees. The toadstool smell of rotting wood and leaf mould hung in the air, thick as Monday's washing. Somewhere a robin sang a requiem for the dying day. Twice we were brought up sharp by a rope of scent stretched taut across the track – the rancid reek of fox.

Back home the gathered branches were snapped into burnable lengths and packed into the log basket. Outside in the dark the frost was fierce. Was that why the vixen up on the hill screamed with such anguish? The curtains were drawn against the night. The room had become a cave of warmth, flickering in the firelight's glow. Wet from the wood, the logs hissed in the flames. The teapot stood by the fire. The hearth gods were happy and so was I. Lopez the tabby came in from the kitchen to curl up on the rug, and together we warmed ourselves in the released energy of ancient sunlight stored up in summers long ago when the oaks were young.

Rose hips in frost

83

JANUARY

5 January
Derwent Ings, North Yorkshire

Heavy with meltwater from the North York Moors, the Derwent flowed under Sutton Bridge faster than a man could walk. The river was high and still rising, and I could not see the bottom. Downstream towards Wheldrake it had crept across the fields to form a huge lake from which the bare superstructure of half-submerged willows leaned like fleets of sunken wrecks.

Snow had fallen in the night. Now the air was like glass and an icy wind ploughed long furrows in the floods which every winter drown the Ings – a 12-mile stretch of rough carrs and watermeadows in the lower Derwent Valley. The wind carried the strange and melancholy sound of swans across the water – not the half-tame swans of lakes in city parks, but Bewick's swans, wild birds from Siberia, for whom these brimming washlands are a vital refuge.

Against the light, in the cold sunshine, the water was as blue as the sea, its bright surface beaded with rafts of duck, its furthest edges flecked with white where the swans were riding. I counted them through binoculars: there were about 90, together with 30 greylag geese and a mixed bag of duck – mostly wigeon and pochard with a scattering of teal and mallard.

Fifteen miles to the south, the tower of Drax B power station raked the sky, four times the height of York Minster. To the east, the distant Wolds gleamed white against the dark snow clouds. There it had snowed steadily until dawn; but the Ings had felt no more than a few brief flurries which now lay as light as frost among the tussocks.

The Derwent is a remarkable stream. Its waters are said to be the cleanest of any lowland river in Britain; and in summer, when it is not

OPPOSITE: *January on the River Stour, Suffolk*

OVERLEAF: *Derwent Ings from Aughton churchyard, North Yorkshire*

85

laden with silt, it runs gin-clear between its low, grassy banks. There are still kingfishers here, and more than thirty kinds of freshwater fish, including salmon and trout, chub, pike, barbel, and perhaps even one or two specimens of that all-but-vanished river cod, the burbot. But the Derwent's real glories are its broad lower reaches, and the Ings which form one of the North Country's last great wetlands. Over the centuries, generations of farmers have installed a system of cloughs, or dykes, to carry away the floodwaters when the river falls in spring, but the land itself has never felt the bite of the plough. Instead, its silt-rich meadows have continued to produce a flush of hay so tall, old farmers used to say, that it would brush a horse's ears. It is a way of farming that has created harmony between man and marsh. It allows marsh orchids and rare water plants to flourish. It provides a hunting ground for barn owls and otters; and in spring, when the floods recede, it becomes a breeding ground for wading birds almost without equal in lowland Britain. Then the tall grass is shot through with the glitter of marsh marigolds, followed by waves of pink ragged robin and the darker crimson heads of great burnet.

Aughton Church

If allowed to continue, the Ings might go on producing summer hay and supporting winter swans for ever: a linear oasis of wet meadows acclaimed by the Nature Conservancy Council as an internationally important site of special scientific interest. But midway through the 1970s progress finally broke the spell which had held the Ings intact for a millennium: the Yorkshire Water Authority built a barrage across the mouth of the Derwent at Barmby to extract drinking water.

In the following winters the floods lay longer on the land, and some hay crops were ruined. Farmers blamed the barrage; the water authority blamed the weather. Whatever the reason, there is no doubt that the Ings have become wetter since the barrage was built, and the shadow of a drainage scheme has hung over the valley ever since. Conservationists fear it could be the beginning of the end for these relic wetlands; though meanwhile the farmers still keep to the old ways, cutting the hay in June and grazing cattle on the aftermath until the silt-enriching floods return.

A magical part of England, then, at all times of the year; but winter is when the Ings come into their own, when the river rises and the land goes under, and wildfowl throng the flooded fields. Bewick's swans are now a common sight. Along with Slimbridge and the Ouse Washes, the Derwent Ings have become one of their main winter refuges. Ospreys have also been seen fishing the floodwaters, and short-eared owls are common. I scanned the fields, hoping for a sight of one; but all I saw were brown hares jinking away through the grass.

At Aughton, lower down the valley, the floodwaters were lapping at the churchyard wall, but the church itself, like the moated manor close by, stood clear of the water on a low, grassy mound. There has probably been a church on this site since Harald Hardrada and his Viking army were slaughtered by the housecarls of King Harold Godwinson, who surprised them not so many miles higher up the Derwent at Stamford Bridge in 1066. The present church is younger by a few centuries, but its squat shape suits the landscape and the low stone tower has a curious carving of a newt on one wall – a fitting symbol for so damp a spot.

Beyond the church, a solitary whooper swan was up-ending for food in the shallows. I walked across a wild meadow purchased by the NCC to protect the abundance of marsh orchids and other wetland plants which grow there, and put up another hare which raced towards the distant willows. Where earlier floods had receded, the waters had dumped an ankle-deep tidemark of sodden chaff. I scooped up a handful and found it to be a mass of wild seeds – an invaluable food source for wintering birds, and one which would be lost if

Newt carved on wall of Aughton Church

ever these undisturbed washlands were drained and ploughed.

Later in the day I came to the village of East Cottingwith to seek out the grave of Snowden Slights, the legendary wildfowler of the Derwent Ings. Carved on his tombstone is a mallard jumping into flight as if startled by the boom of Slights' ancient punt gun, silent these past seventy years. Of all the graves in the tiny churchyard, his lies closest to his beloved Ings, whose waters glittered over the wall, just past the Blue Bell Inn. The inscription on the stone reads: 'In Memory of Snowden Slights, Wildfowler, of East Cottingwith, June 14, 1829–April 15, 1913.'

His armoury was dispersed long ago, but the legend still lingers in the Derwent Valley. Wildfowling with punt and gun was still quite new to the Derwent when Slights was born. By the time he was nine he had already left school to join his father on regular punt-gunning forays. At fifteen he was a dead shot, a hefty, big-boned lad who thought nothing of walking to Pocklington market twice a week with a sack of dead ducks – a round trip of 18 miles. In summer he worked as a basket weaver, and when he married he invested all his small capital in an osier bed to grow the supple willows which are the raw materials of the basket maker's craft. But soon afterwards, disaster struck: a freak winter destroyed his osiers and left him penniless. Fortunately the ice and floods which had brought him ruin also provided his salvation. Huge flocks of wildfowl came pouring out of the sky to settle among the flooded fields: wild swans from Russia, packs of geese from the frozen east coast estuaries, and all kinds of duck. Every day during that terrible freeze he lay in his low, grey punt, the hoar frost crusted on his corduroy coat, creeping like an old dog otter across the misty waters. And every day his great muzzle-loading punt gun boomed out over the fen, drenching the huddled flocks with its blizzard of lead.

And so he kept not only himself and his family from starvation but also found himself on the road to becoming the king of the Yorkshire punt gunners. Photographs taken around the turn of the century, and now in the Yorkshire Museum at York, reveal him as a great, gaunt oak of a man, his face deep-etched by the hard marsh winters.

Those were the days when anything that flew was fair game, and Snowden laid into the local wildfowl and other birdlife with a determination that would have appalled present-day birdlovers. You could buy a pink-footed goose for three shillings and sixpence, bitterns were two shillings each, kingfishers one shilling and a jack snipe sixpence. Once he had got within 35 yards of his target he seldom missed. On one occasion he hit 24 mallard and 20 wigeon with a single shot, though that does not seem quite so remarkable when you look at the artillery he used – some of his guns had barrels as big as drainpipes. His biggest, a giant muzzle loader built in Beverley for his father, weighed 140 lb and had a barrel 10 feet long that could throw 16 lb of lead shot. The guns were mounted in an open, clinker-built pinewood punt 17 feet long with a three-foot beam. When fully laden the gunwales cleared the water by a mere six inches.

He was still wildfowling when he was eighty, two years before his death. His had been a tough and solitary life, lying for hours on end in his punt, often soaked, frequently frozen (once he was found with his corduroys frozen on him and carried home, stiff as a board, to be thawed out by his fireside). Yet he is on record as having said: 'If I had my life to come over again I would still be a wildfowler, but I would go in for it properly.' God help the geese if he had.

By a strange twist of fate his old killing ground, a wild waste of flooded watermeadows called Wheldrake Ings, is now a nature reserve, bought by the Yorkshire Naturalists' Trust in 1971 to protect the wintering wildfowl that Snowden Slights once butchered. I walked out to the hide in the middle of the Ings, following the river where it flowed silently past stricken ranks of fallen hemlock. Wrens ticked among the brittle stems, and a wind of Siberian intensity hissed over the fields. In this last hour of the day the low sun poured towards the waiting distance, throwing giant shadows to where a screaming flock of black-headed gulls were gathered. Nearby, lapwings and golden plovers were feeding. Further off were more Bewick's swans with a few greylag geese and a vast congregation of wigeon. Beyond, in the east, the snowy Wolds shone across the vale, whiter than ever in the evening light, while dark ranges of snow clouds moved down the North Sea behind them. As flight time came, the sky filled with chevrons of whistling wigeon. Out on the Ings the gulls turned pink in the last rays of the sun, until they looked more like the flamingos of Kenya's Rift Valley lakes than the roosting flocks of a Yorkshire marsh.

Short-eared owl

14 January
Tregaron, Dyfed

Cors Caron in January is a sombre place. Its colours are the muted shades of winter reeds and tussock sedge, a waste of willow carr and heather relieved only by the treacherous green of sphagnum beds, and sometimes by the thinner branches of the birch trees which in certain lights glow like port wine.

LEFT: *Hen harrier over Cors Caron, Dyfed*
BELOW: *Polecat*

A raven watched me from a fence post. Far out in the emptiness of the bog, under a sky heavy with the threat of snow, shaggy ponies were grazing at the edge of a thicket, for all the world like the prehistoric horses of Neolithic Britain. There was no shelter from the wind. The hills of mid-Wales lay along the horizon, as dull as bruises. With fingers frozen inside two pairs of gloves I scanned the far side of the bog through binoculars, and picked up a herd of twelve whooper swans sailing on a gleam of water. Nothing else moved.

Some twenty thousand years ago the tongue of an Ice Age glacier scoured this wide basin in the Welsh hills. Later, as Britain grew warmer and the ice retreated, a boulder moraine blocked the valley, causing a shallow lake to form; and in time, when the lake silted up, Cors Caron – the Great Bog of Tregaron – was born.

Cors Caron is a perfect example of a raised mire – a type of bog which is fast disappearing from lowland Britain. Its vital ingredient is sphagnum moss: a botanical sponge so successful at mopping up water and nutrients that it forms giant carpets which create their own acid environment and in time transform the original fen into true bog. As the mosses die they sink to the bottom, forming a thick undercarpet of peat which eventually causes the bog to rise above the surrounding land. Yet instead of drying out and draining away, the raised bog continues to grow, swelling with every winter's rains and constantly laying down peat, until after seven thousand years its domed surface may have risen up to 30 feet above the original lake bed.

Legend has it that beneath Cors Caron lies a buried city called Maesllyn. If so, it has never given up its secrets. Yet the bog itself has been generous for centuries, providing peat for hearth fires, dry rushes for stable bedding and grazing for stock. The peat was cut in early summer, then stacked to dry until early autumn when it was hauled out by horse and cart before rising water levels made the tracks impassable. Peat cutting had ceased by 1960. Today, wintering snipe and teal haunt the flooded diggings, and the Great Bog of Tregaron is a national nature reserve. Willow carr has invaded the wettest hollows and spread along the low-lying depression known as the lagg, which encircles the bog. Here, too, are rushes, reed canary-grass and other water-loving plants, including the rotted hulks of wild iris; but as the mire rises and becomes more acid, cotton-grass and purple moor-grass appear, and are in turn replaced by deer-grass, heather and bog rosemary, tussock sedge and heaving peat hummocks, with scatterings of gnarled birch on the drier ridges.

There are otters in the valley, for the River Teifi flows through the middle of the bog and is full of eels as well as the migrant salmon and trout which move upstream to spawn each year. Cors Caron is also a stronghold for polecats, which prowl among its reeds and tussocks, preying on voles and sniffing out nests of snipe and redshank. Other birds which breed here in summer are mallard, curlew, reed bunting and even a few red grouse. Throughout the year, buzzard, sparrow-hawk, red kite and barn owl patrol the reserve; in winter they are joined by hen harrier, short-eared owl, peregrine and merlin.

Once it was possible to watch the birds from the railway which linked Tregaron and Lampeter with Aberystwyth to the north and Carmarthen to the south. Where it crossed the bog, the line floated on a raft of wooden faggots and bales of wool. But in December 1963 heavy floods breached the track and it was never repaired. Since then the line has been taken up and the track is now a footpath for visitors to the reserve, skirting Allt ddu Farm until after about a mile it leads to an observation tower by the Afon Fflur.

My guide and companion on this bitterly cold day was Roger Lovegrove, a former physical education teacher who now works for the Royal Society for the Protection of Birds. For more than two decades he has been one of their most steadfast guardians, watching over the welfare of the birds of Wales from the RSPB regional headquarters at Newtown in Powys. A tall, lean man, his face fur-rowed by long days out of doors, he bubbles with energy, eloquence and enthusiasm, and his knowledge of Wales and its birds is unsur-passed. He knows every inch of country, from the oaks of Gwenffrwd, where redstarts and pied flycatchers breed, to the winter kite roosts and lonely upland hunting grounds of the last Welsh merlins.

The tower shook in the wind as we climbed into the hide and looked out across the valley. Someone was shooting in the fields on the other side, and the sound reverberated over the bog, sending up flights of mallard and a pair of fast-moving smaller duck which Lovegrove at once identified as teal. We scanned the skyline with our binoculars, hoping to pick up a merlin, but in vain. We checked each distant stump and fence post, looking for short-eared owls, but found none. Then Lovegrove's sharp eyes spotted a flicker of movement low over the willow carr. I swung my glasses to where he was pointing, and as the circle of distance swam into focus I found a hen harrier, a beautiful, ring-tailed female sailing on her long wings among the stunted trees.

Suddenly a swifter shape shot into view, causing the harrier to rise sharply in alarm. 'Peregrine,' whispered Lovegrove excitedly. Even at so great a distance I could make out the hawk's barbaric mask as it chased the much larger harrier into the sky. The peregrine appeared to be playing, revelling in its supreme mastery of the air, whereas the

Bog of Tregaron - Jan/84.

♀ (imm)? Hen Harrier

beating hard
- high up.

legs rarely
visible
even low down

harrier – so elegant and so effortless when we had first seen her – was now made to seem clumsy by comparison as she struggled to avoid his sudden swoops. 'He's pulling his punches,' grinned Lovegrove; and, sure enough, the peregrine peeled away as if tiring of its sport and began to ring up until it was a mere black star high under the racing snow clouds. Then its wings closed and it slid down the sky until its stoop became a monumental fall to earth, a black wedge flinging downwards too fast to follow; I lost him against a darkness of hills and could only guess at his whereabouts by the shrapnel bursts of panic-stricken lapwings which blew up in his wake across the distant fields.

A peregrine aloft is like no other bird. It carries with it a constant aura of imminent drama, and so long as it remains in the air it possesses this extraordinary power to dominate the horizons. So it was at Tregaron. When the peregrine had gone, the bog fell silent again, waiting for the snow which had threatened all morning and was sure to come soon.

The harrier did not return, so we walked back to the car and tried to thaw out with a flask of hot coffee and sandwiches. Then we left Cors Caron and headed north through Pontrhydfendigaid and Pontrhydygroes, following the River Ystwyth into one of the loveliest valleys in mid-Wales. We passed Hafod church and at last came to a high lane among lonely hills with thick woods of oak and larch reaching towards us, and the Ystwyth writhing in silver coils through the meadows below. Squalls of hail swept the hills – to be followed by a strange, granular snow that dusted the summits and settled like hoar frost in the lane. We parked in a lay-by looking down into the vertiginous valley, and waited for the red kites which Lovegrove knew would soon come drifting in to roost in the oaks beneath us.

The return of the red kite is a success story for British conservation, and for the RSPB in particular. It was not always a rare bird. In Elizabethan times red kites were regular scavengers in the streets of London, and they remained common until the late eighteenth century. But then followed the age of intensive game preservation, in which all predators were regarded as vermin, to be killed by any means. Easy to shoot, even simpler to poison, the red kite never stood a chance. By 1870 it had gone from England. Thirty years later the last Scottish red kites had been wiped out, leaving the hills of central Wales as the bird's last refuge. Here at the turn of the century a handful of pairs survived among the remote and unkeepered valleys, and clung on long enough for more enlightened views to prevail.

Since then, aided by round-the-clock protection at nest sites in the breeding season, the red kite has clawed its way back from the brink. Its recovery has been painfully slow, but today it is no longer the rarest

OPPOSITE: *Hen harrier sketched at Cors Caron, Dyfed*

breeding bird of prey in Wales; that dubious privilege has passed to the merlin. Yet the red kite still breeds only in Wales, and its presence here is the motivating spark which gives these hills their tension. In kite country there is always a tingling sense of anticipation. The eye scours the hilltops, yearning for a glimpse of that rakish silhouette, the long wings bent against the pluck of wind, and a fanned fork tail – the kite's true trademark – deep-etched against the winter sky.

Now, singly and in pairs, the first birds began to arrive, sailing and circling over the head of the valley. By day they hunt alone or in pairs, scavenging over the hills for dead sheep or rabbits, sometimes travelling up to 15 miles but always returning to their communal winter roost among the sheltering oaks. At one point I had six red kites in view. Later I counted nine spiralling together. They flew in the teeth of the wind, heedless of the slanting snow which reduced the more distant birds to wraiths. Some passed within 50 feet of where we sat, and one came so close that I could see every detail of its plumage, as if in a measured drawing. Its body and wing coverts were brown and tawny

Red kites flying to roost, central Wales

98

like November oaks. The red tail drew its colour from the dead bracken, and the head and wing patches were as one with the hills under their dusting of snow. And still they came, rocking and swaying on crooked wings, riding in on the blizzard as dusk began to fall. We counted at least thirty: one quarter of all the red kites of Wales. Even Roger Lovegrove was thrilled. 'In twenty years of birdwatching in Wales that is the most I have seen in a single day,' he said.

20 January

Powerstock, Dorset

Last night was intensely cold. There were frost ferns on the windows when I awoke, and, although the south-facing slopes were green again by lunchtime, frost lingered all day in the sunless valley bottoms where rank weeds stood stiff with rime and every hoofprint bore a brittle shell of ice.

A buzzard was mewing over Welcome Hill as we followed the *Buzzard* stream down the valley, hoping to find the year's first snowdrops. At any season of the year the stream is a source of endless pleasure with its dippers and grey wagtails, its summer jungles of butterbur and exquisite demoiselle flies. It has its beginnings at the foot of Eggardon, dribbling out of the heavy clays which nourish the oaks of Powerstock Common; but as it progresses it is swollen by other rivulets which come gurgling down from ditches and combes. By the time it flows past Whetley orchard (flooding the road after heavy rain), it has acquired its first small trout, and by Powerstock it has collected its first stone bridge. Eventually it becomes the Mangerton Brook, a tributary of the River Brit, which empties into West Bay harbour.

Below Powerstock the stream is embanked with alders whose upper branches now glowed lustrous bronze as we made our way down the valley in weak sunshine, passing through a succession of overgrown copses and wet, rushy meadows which had frozen underfoot in places. Kingcups bloom here in spring, followed in June by the mauve spikes of the beautiful southern marsh orchid, *Dactylorhiza praetermissa*; but in winter the glory of the valley is its wild snowdrops which grow in profusion along the banks. Normally we look for them on 18 January – my daughter's birthday – but this year they were late; and today we found only a dozen white buds.

Compensation came when we startled a large dog fox as we returned home along the bridleway. He was in fine condition: his winter coat

Red fox

was at its thickest, a rich red-gold with a hoary dusting of white-tipped hairs on the rump and a bold white tip on his bushy tail. He stared at us with amber eyes, then streaked off through the bracken and away up the hill. We caught his scent, rank and feral, as we squeezed through a gap in the hedge and plunged in pursuit – only to find him calmly watching us from the top of the hill with another fox beside him.

As soon as they had moved on again we scrambled through wet bracken to follow them up the grassy lynchets to the hilltop. As we came over the crest an extraordinary sight met our eyes. There, less than a hundred yards away, chasing each other over the grass, were now *four* foxes. They were so preoccupied with each other that they did not appear to notice our breathless arrival, and we were able to watch for several minutes until at last they dived into a dense blackthorn thicket from which emerged the harsh, weird cries of their mating.

I could only guess that what we had witnessed was a vixen on heat which had attracted three suitors – including the dog fox we had met in the lane – and that one of them had at last succeeded in coupling with her. If their mating was successful, there would be cubs by mid-March.

Suddenly winter no longer seemed invincible. The new year was slowly gathering momentum. The days were still short, but the mating foxes and the returning snowdrops were signs that the country-side was at last emerging from its sleep.

23 January
Stour Valley, Suffolk

And nigh this toppling reed, still as the dead
The great pike lies, the murderous patriarch
Watching the waterpit sheer-shelving dark,
Where through the plash his lithe bright vassals thread.
EDMUND BLUNDEN

Suffolk lay silent under a leaden sky. Last night six inches of snow smothered the Stour Valley. Later it rained, reducing the pristine fields to crust, though a dull carapace of ice still covered Borley Mill pool. But now, as I followed the river downstream to Brundon, the air held a hint of more snow to come.

The Stour Valley is low and undulating country where distance is measured in 100-acre fields and horizons are marked by lonely church towers. Between Long Melford and Sudbury it becomes Gainsborough's England, home of the painter, who was born at Sudbury in 1727. But today, under snow, its wintry landscapes were as bleak as a Breughel.

The Stour rises at the border of Suffolk and Cambridgeshire on Wratting Common, where the London clays run up against the spring line of the East Anglian chalk; and for most of the 80-odd miles down to its estuary beyond Manningtree it is willow country. Commonest is the crack willow, *Salix fragilis*, whose twigs come away with a snap when pulled; but the wet alluvial soils are also ideal for the majestic white willow, which can drink 400 gallons a day when fully grown, and its close relative the bat willow, whose solid, silky wood is carved into cricket bats.

Summer and winter, the Stour is a cold river; its temperature seldom varies more than a few degrees. Recent floods had left sodden tide-marks of straw and dead wood along the banks and the river was still high. Under the trees it was a dark bottle green, swollen with meltwater from the streaming ditches. It is a good river to fish, clean and slow, with deep pools and long swims between rippling mare's tails of submerged weed. Somewhere down there furtive chub would be moving, heavy and blunt-mouthed among the drowned tree roots, with fat carp and bronze tench rooting for bloodworms in the muddy bottom like pigs after acorns; and maybe, lurking among the reeds, the shadow of a hungry pike.

Best for pike are the spots where the old mill races have scoured pools up to 30 feet deep in places; and in one such hole lives the legendary pike known as the Old Man of Brundon. The miller who lived at Borley Mill until 1970 would often talk of the 'gurt luce' (Suffolk dialect for a great pike) which patrolled the river between here and Brundon. Pike have a fondness for cruising just below the surface; and sometimes the miller, half glimpsing a sudden movement in the water, would turn in time to see a huge, recumbent shape, like a dappled log, sinking back into the darkness.

In 1971 the mill changed hands; it was bought by Rupert Brown, a book designer, who dismissed rumours of a giant pike as local folklore. But the following year he found a dead swan floating in the mill pool. It was headless and had an enormous bite on its thigh. 'No otter could have left such marks,' said Brown. 'They could have been made only by the jaws of a big fish with eye teeth as long as an alsatian's.' Since then he has seen the monster on several occasions; and once he met a white-faced angler, his tackle smashed, who thought he must have hooked a seal.

So the legend of the Old Man of Brundon has continued to grow,

OVERLEAF: *Stour Valley, Suffolk, under snow*

The Old Man of Brundon

while the fish itself, heavier and more cunning with each passing year, is now thought to weigh close on 40 lb. It can be recognized by a split pectoral fin on its left side. 'That had to be the Old Man,' the miller would exclaim. 'I see'd the cleft fin.' But no fisherman had ever succeeded in landing him. Now he was a veteran, maybe half a century old, which meant that he had probably been patrolling this same stretch of river since before I was born. It was a strange thought.

I had first heard about the Old Man of Brundon the previous summer, when I had come down to Borley to write an article for the *Sunday Times Magazine* about a new angling book which Rupert Brown was designing with Martin Knowelden, the wildlife artist. As a fish painter, Knowelden is supreme. With pencil or paintbrush he can capture a fish better than anyone, and preserve it in oils with every reed and ripple of its mysterious world intact. He had seen the Old Man that spring. 'He was huge,' he said. 'Come back in the winter and we'll try and catch him.'

I had no illusions that we would succeed. Nor did I particularly want to see the legend reduced to a varnished carcass, stuffed with sawdust and staring glassy-eyed from a trophy case. But regardless of the swollen river and the snow that had begun to fall afresh, Martin was determined that we should fish for pike. So, legs entombed in wellingtons and waterproofs, we trudged along the bank until we found a pool where a small brook joined the river. There, Martin knew, the water was a good seven feet deep and the far bank bristled with bulrushes, whose submerged stems offered perfect cover for pike.

We carried two rods. One was 11 feet long, a slender thing of hollow glass. That would be used to ledger or dead-bait for the Old Man, using snap tackle on a wire trace, with two treble hooks and a sprat from the freezer. The other was a nine-foot glass spinning rod with a plug painted to resemble a small pickerel. If the plug was jerked through the murky water a pike might sense the uneven vibrations and mistake the movements for those of a sick or wounded fish.

Martin took the big rod first and cast the dead-bait downstream with a finely judged flick that dropped it in about five feet of water, so that the sprat would lie on the bottom below a small red pike bob. Then he slackened the ratchet on the reel and set the rod to rest.

Now began the long wait, during which I learned the infinite patience of the dedicated pike man, and tried to forget my frozen feet. The river flowed past in slow, viscous coils and I watched the red bob as if mesmerized, willing it to dip down under the weight of a fish; but it never moved. Gradually the life of the river returned to normal. A moorhen emerged from a ditch and padded across the white fields on outsize feet. A dabchick came drifting down with the current, diving and reappearing lower downstream. A kingfisher settled briefly on a low branch, glittering like an electric spark before whirring downriver with a shrill whistle. 'Angling is a marvellous way of observing wildlife,' said Martin. 'On a walk, all you see is a circle of fearful or fleeing birds and animals. But once you sit still, life goes on again as if you weren't there.'

We sat hunched like herons, but the cold bit to the marrow until we were forced to stand up and move around to keep warm. No luck with the dead-bait, so Martin took up the smaller spinning rod. An hour passed, lost in total absorption, in the repetitive flick of the rod's end, the mechanical winding in of the plug. By now the snow was falling steadily in fat, wet flakes, shutting out the distant hedgerows. My thoughts began to wander. I thought of the first time I had come to Borley. It had been early summer, with the smell of may blossom drifting across the meadows in sultry tides, and I had sat on the bank and watched the tarnished gleam of shoaling chub as they cruised in the sun-warmed shallows below the mill.

I thought of the carp I had eaten last winter in Yugoslavia, skewered on a willow stick, basted with olive oil and cooked over the embers of a wood fire in the marshes of Hutavo Blato; and the giant carp in our own British waters, and the stoical fanatics who fish for them by night, alone in the immense silence of the dark. I thought of the pike with its shovel snout and wolfish teeth, every inch a predator.

And still no warning movement from the small red bob. I tried to guess what was happening in that secret world beneath the surface as the rich, oily taint of sprat drifted down with the current. Somewhere, surely, a pike must be lurking, cold eyes unblinking. Perhaps the Old Man himself, heavy with the weight of years, watching, waiting. . . .

When it happened, it was a total surprise; my daydreams were shattered by the reel's urgent whirring. Already Martin had dived for the rod and was stripping off more line as the tip jumped and the bob went under. When the line slackened briefly, he tightened the ratchet and struck once, against the pull, setting the barbs in the gristle of the fish's jaw. At once the rod curved taut as the pike took off in a violent dash in an effort to rid itself of the tormenting hook.

Three minutes passed. The fish was tiring. As it lost the power of its caudal muscles it began to roll in the water, and for the first time we could see it, a greenish blossoming of light, a heavy body swinging like a scythe blade, and a broad, flapping tail. It wasn't the Old Man of Brundon, but it was a good fish all the same. There was a thrashing and a shaking, and then Martin had the keep net under, and up she came: a

Coots on frozen river

fresh, deep-bellied hen. An 11-pounder, we discovered later, and in Martin's words 'a welcome addition to the deep-freeze'. Carefully he removed the hooks with surgical forceps. A swift *coup de grâce* with the priest – and it was all over.

24 January
Stour Valley, Suffolk

The sound of the mill race woke me this morning. Outside in the snow, blackbirds and fieldfares were squabbling over scabbed and rotting windfall apples. If the cold continues it will be hard for the birds. The smallest are often the first to suffer – it is thought that three quarters of all British wrens perished in the winter of 1962. The same freeze also killed 85 per cent of all Welsh kingfishers; and in an earlier winter, in 1947, the rare bearded tit was all but wiped out, with only three pairs surviving the weeks of arctic weather.

Rupert and Martin both keep lurchers, and after breakfast we set out with them to look for hares. Both men are keen field naturalists who care deeply about the countryside and its wildlife, and yet they see nothing wrong in hunting for the pot. 'That's really why we keep the dogs,' said Rupert. 'It's good to bring home a hare for supper. But we also enjoy the beauty of working a running dog, its strength and stamina and intelligence – and in going out with them you, too, become a true hunter. They become an extension of your own senses, so that when you walk the fields with a dog at your side the anticipation is electric.'

Martin's lurcher – he doesn't like you to call him a long-dog – is named Tig because of his colour, which is a rusty, tigerish brindle. He is deep-chested and weighs 65 lb. 'A large, indescribably shaggy brute who looks as if he has slept all night under a pile of old teabags,' said Martin proudly. Rupert's dog, Pye, on the other hand, is smooth-haired, with the long, fine-tuned legs and swaybacked racing frame of a true greyhound, and is altogether more aristocratic than the villainous and untidy Tig. 'Pye's part Saluki, part Nureyev,' declared Rupert, 'the only dog I've known to catch a partridge in mid-air.' Together the two dogs make a good team. Now, overjoyed at being liberated for the morning, they romped and fawned and rolled in the snow until Tig's coarse coat was an unkempt rug of wet, bristly points.

Snow had buried the ploughlands, obliterating every trace of furrow and stubble. We were the sole moving figures in a world without

Brown hare

colour, its whiteness relieved only by thin, black scrolls of hedge and a smudge of bare trees along the Stour. Snipe flew up where the ditches had not yet frozen, but silently, without their usual scraping cries of alarm. The dogs did not bark and the only sounds were the plaintive whispers of meadow pipits driven before us over the snowbound fields. A wind began to rise, coming off the icy fields with a bitter edge. 'That's what we call a lazy wind in East Anglia,' said Martin, slipping easily into the slow Suffolk way of speaking. 'That's too lazy to goo round yer; so it goo straight through yer.'

When we saw a pair of hares two fields' lengths away, Martin quietly called the dogs to heel and put them on a short leash. We advanced obliquely at a crouch, seeking dead ground which would hide us until we had halved the distance; but as soon as we had breasted the rise and become visible again, the hares were running like the wind.

The dogs were slipped and ran utterly mute, scudding over the fields with the snow flying up behind them. The hares stopped briefly and froze, balancing on their hind legs, big ears cocked; then split and ran in opposite directions. For a moment the dogs were confused – long enough to win the hares a few precious yards. But then both dogs were on the heels of the same hare as it jinked away. Sometimes it seemed as if it would collide with one dog as it veered away to avoid the other. Now they were running back towards us, and at last the hare had begun to pull away from its pursuers, gaining ground as it took advantage of the long rise. As it sprinted past us it was so close that I could hear the thud of its pads in the snow.

Suddenly Pye was down in a tumble of legs and unable to rise. At once Rupert and Martin were running towards him, afraid that he had broken a leg in the hidden furrows; but luckily it was nothing worse than a sprain. Tig, meanwhile, had run on alone, still chasing the hare; but by now it had swum the Belchamp Brook and was streaking away into the next parish. Only then, realizing that he had been beaten, did Tig stop and return with lolling tongue and heaving chest, looking somewhat crestfallen and more untidy than ever. At full stretch he had been as lithe and as beautiful to watch as a cheetah hunting gazelle on the high plains of East Africa. But my heart was with the hare and I was relieved to see it get away, although I did not tell Martin. He was making a fuss of his lurcher. 'Tig, you old monster, you,' he said. 'You're so ugly you're almost beautiful.'

Common snipe

FEBRUARY

13 February
Powerstock, Dorset

Three degrees of frost this morning; yet by lunchtime it was warm enough to sit outside. The false spring sunshine had also brought out a buff-tailed bumblebee, which was busily squeezing itself into the open mouths of yellow crocuses. Here in the south, on bright days such as this, the queens are often to be seen among the early-flowering primroses, or blundering along the banks in search of abandoned voles' nests in which to start new colonies.

I walked down the valley, following the stream under awnings of hazel catkins dusted with pollen, to find the snowdrops in full bloom. It is a sight which never fails to move me. Of all our wild flowers, they are the purest, the most ethereal, chaste and shade-loving: white bells for Candlemas. They lay now in deep drifts and pockets under the trees, flowering beside the stream all the way to West Milton.

How they first came to be there it is impossible to say. The snowdrop was not recognized as a wild plant in Britain until the eighteenth century, and it is only here in the West Country that it flourishes naturally in our damp February woods and river valleys. Perhaps these had begun as fugitives from Nettlecombe: garden escapes gone over the wall to take root in the waterside humus below. From there, swept away by winter floods, the bulbs must have spread easily, forming new colonies downstream.

The snowdrops were not the only signs of winter's yielding. Thrushes pealed from the hedgetops, expending precious energy to proclaim their breeding territories. In the banks below, the spotted leaves of cuckoo pint were emerging. Even the iron-grey elder bushes had begun to put out new beetroot-coloured leaf buds, and the first OPPOSITE: *Frogs' spawn*

BELOW and RIGHT: *Dorset snowdrops*

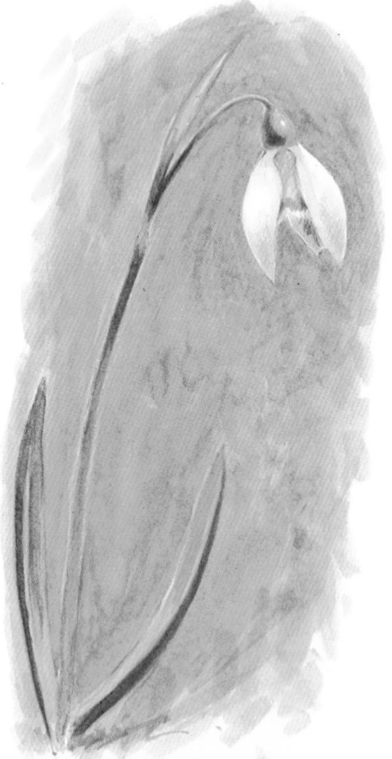

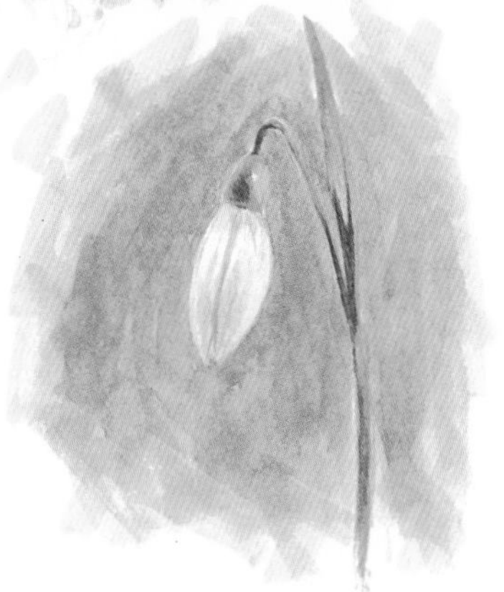

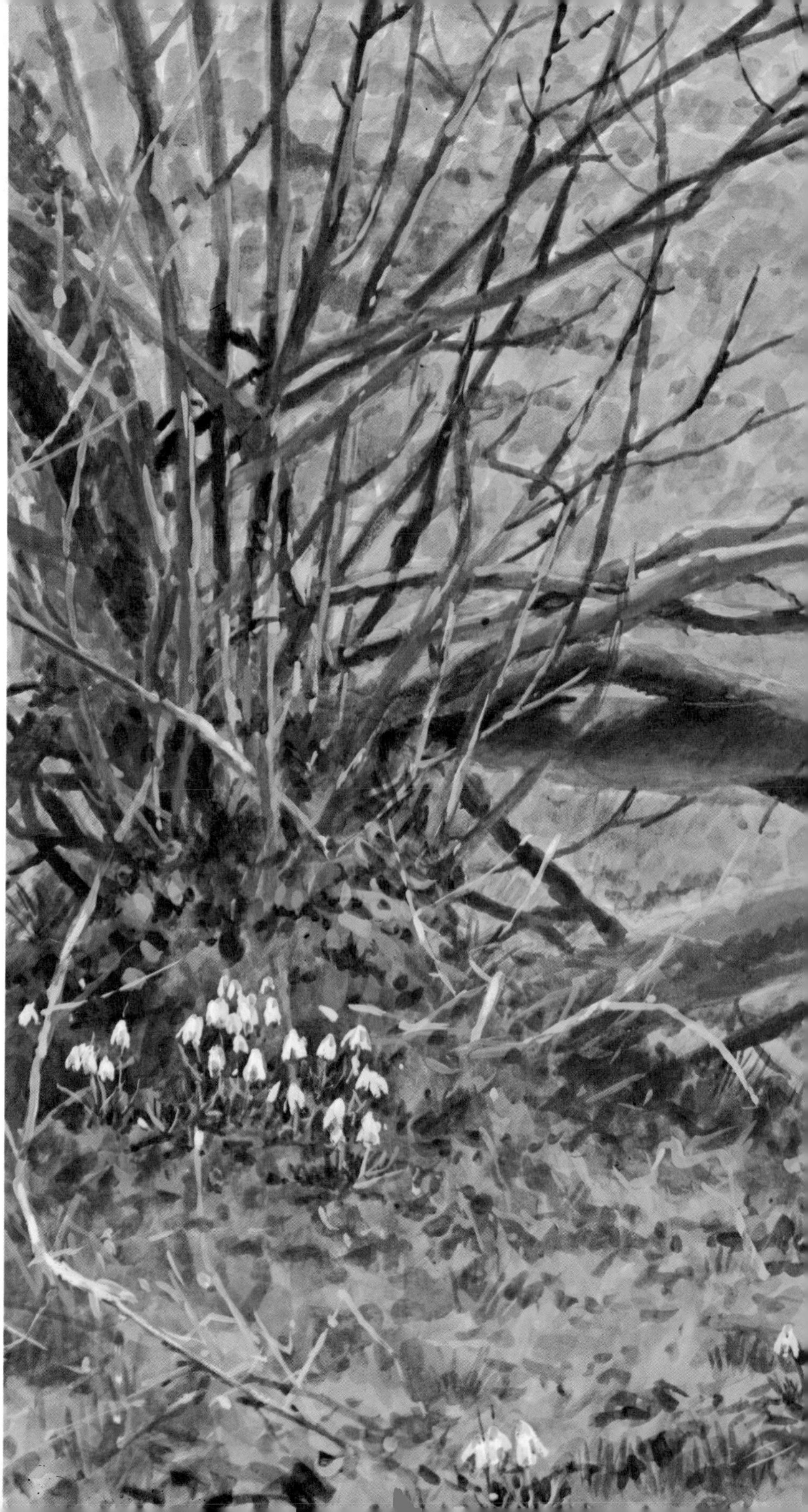

constellations of lesser celandines had appeared in the lanes, rayed like the sun whose growing strength had coaxed them to open. Even more than the snowdrops, they signified a return to longer hours of daylight as the earth set its face away from winter. They are sensitive flowers, never opening until the sun is well above the horizon, closing at the first hint of rain, and shutting tight again long before nightfall. But from then until the end of spring they would shine from every sheltered bankside and south-facing lynchet.

Midway between Powerstock and West Milton the stream slides down the sluice of a mill mentioned in the Domesday Book. The mill vanished long ago, leaving only its mossy foundation stones and the course of the old leat, now reduced to a boggy depression lined with rushes. In spring, marsh marigolds flower there, and in summer yellow flags; but in winter the leat becomes a chain of shallow rainwater pools – a favourite place for spawning frogs.

I searched among the mats of watercress and floating sweet-grass, and sure enough the widest pools were filled with buoyant mounds of jelly, each transparent globule containing a black speck of life. There was no sign of the breeding frogs themselves. They would have emerged from hibernation some time in January, the males quietly croaking as they sought a mate. Once they had paired off in the ponds they would swim in tandem for days, even weeks, the female clasped in the male's cold embrace until suddenly, in the cheerless light of a February dawn, she would release her spawn, shedding as many as three thousand eggs for the male to fertilize. The previous year we had taken a small handful home in a jamjar and watched them grow from sooty, gold-speckled tadpoles into miniature froglets which my daughter had then returned to the marsh. Now the year had come full circle, although the frogs we had released would not return to breed for another four springs.

Beyond the old leat the land belongs to Everard Marsh, who farms 50 acres of steep hillside and lynchet, supplementing his income by providing bed and breakfast for holiday visitors. A board hangs at the top of the lane, offering accommodation in several languages: 'Fremdenzimmer . . . Chambres à louer' – a sign of changing times in Dorset, where cars with European registration plates are now a common sight in our summer lanes. But winter is a time for chores in the fields, and today Everard was out laying his boundary hedge above the road. In an age when most of our lanes are laid waste with heavy-duty flails that leave a trail of mangled stumps and pulverized twigs it was heartening to see someone who still cares for his hedges, cutting them cleanly with a billhook and laying them by hand in the old manner.

Everard Marsh hedge-laying

The hedge – a mixture of blackthorn, hazel and pollard ash – was last cut about twelve years earlier. Everard doesn't care much for mechanical flails because, he says, you need to use them every year; whereas a well-laid hedge trimmed by hand should not need cutting for at least another seven years. The first job is to clear out all the dead and unwanted rubbish: brambles, ivy, old man's beard. If there is a ditch at the bottom, the sludge must be cleared and thrown up onto the hedgebank as ready-made compost to enrich the tired soil. Next, for the hedge's horizontal strength, Everard chooses a tall, upright sapling: ash and hazel are the most pliant. Using a billhook he chops it diagonally, not all the way through but deep enough to force it to yield without breaking when laid flat. These horizontals – Everard calls them plushers – are then plashed, or woven, one among the others with short spars pushed through at regular intervals to hold them down. Always when laying a hedge he works uphill, so that the rain will not run down the growing branches and freeze at night, killing the growing tips.

The result is a living, self-renewing fence, a stockproof shelter costing no more than the labour of its upkeep, a poor man's larder of nuts and berries, and an unofficial nature reserve. Every hedge is, in effect, a linear wood: a lifeline for innumerable species of wild plants and creatures who could not survive in the open fields. Many of the hedges which we have come to think of as permanent features of the English countryside are no older than the Enclosures of the eighteenth century; but others go back at least to the Dark Ages, and are the surviving boundaries of Bronze Age farms or Saxon parishes. A rough yardstick devised by Dr Max Hooper (an eminent plant ecologist) to estimate the age of a hedge is to count the number of shrub species growing in each 30-yard length and allow a hundred years for each one. On that basis many of the hedges around Powerstock have stood here since the Conquest.

In my lifetime Britain has lost more than half a million miles of hedgerows in the drive for more efficient farming. Others may not long survive the annual mangling under the flails of the heavy-duty cutters. But a hedge like Everard's will avoid the false economies of fencing. Cut and laid just once in a decade, there is no reason why it should not continue to harbour its rabbits, flowers and finches' nests for another nine hundred years.

Pussy willow

15 February
Powerstock, Dorset

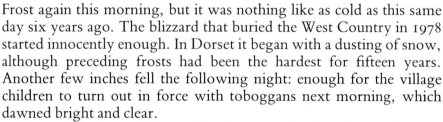

Frost again this morning, but it was nothing like as cold as this same day six years ago. The blizzard that buried the West Country in 1978 started innocently enough. In Dorset it began with a dusting of snow, although preceding frosts had been the hardest for fifteen years. Another few inches fell the following night: enough for the village children to turn out in force with toboggans next morning, which dawned bright and clear.

The weekend was different. The sky turned leaden, the wind swung round to the east and at lunchtime on Saturday it began to snow again – not soft, fat, Christmas flakes but a pitiless blast of frost-sharpened powder which settled fast. In the evening, friends were due for dinner from Beaminster, five miles away. They couldn't make it; the roads were blocked.

On Sunday morning we awoke to a scene of pure Antarctica. Five feet of snow lay against the door. Outside, it was impossible to walk even 20 yards without floundering waist deep, so I took down my skies from the attic and set out to explore. The high winds had flung great drifts against walls and hedgerows. On hills and bank tops huge frozen cornices hung like Atlantic breakers in mid-curl. The sunken lanes had filled so deeply with snow that I could cross from hedge to hedge with the road 15 feet beneath. Cars lay buried where they had been abandoned, only their radio aerials visible.

At one spot on the downs above us the snow was so deep that it was possible to sit on top of the telegraph poles. In beleaguered Bridport the townsfolk built snowmen in the middle of the High Street. Snowbergs floated in the harbour at West Bay, where pounding seas had punched a 60-yard hole in the promenade, and over everything lay the unaccustomed silence of a world without traffic.

In the afternoon a force ten storm was blowing off Portland Bill and driving still more snow across an Ice Age Dorset. That night foxes and roe deer ran hungry through the village gardens; their prints were clear to see next day. Small birds perished where they hid in hedges. Robins and blackbirds pecked ravenously at garden scraps. Snipe and lapwing, normally the wariest of birds, lost all fear of men and fed on a farmyard dunghill where snow had melted on the Knap. Aunt Isobel, then the oldest resident in the village, had seen nothing like it in all her ninety years.

Now television and radio bulletins began to sketch in the full effects of what an emergency edition of the local paper described as 'The Great White Straitjacket' . . . the entire West Country paralysed; schools closed; roads stopped up by mammoth drifts; Yeovil, Dorchester and Barnstaple cut off; Dartmoor and Exmoor reduced to Siberias. Telephone calls to friends filled in local gaps. Forage was dropped by helicopter for animals marooned on Eggardon Hill, whose Iron Age earthworks held 20 feet of snow; dead sheep were being dug out and fed to pigs; thousands of gallons of milk had to be poured down the drain. In short, it spelt heartbreak and near-disaster for many Dorset farmers.

Like most villagers, we survived comfortably and were grateful. There was no lack of food or fuel; bread was home-baked; milk was being given away. It was like Christmas as it should be, stripped of movement and greed. We dug out an elderly lady whose cottage was half buried. A neighbour ran a samaritan errand on skis, taking pills to a housebound arthritis sufferer in the next valley.

By Wednesday the thaw had set in. Meltwater was pouring off the hills and tractors were working round the clock as farmers cleared the lanes with yard scrapers in a desperate battle to get their milk to market. Helicopters grounded by fog the day before now resumed their mercy missions. Flooding was the next fear, for the sodden ground could absorb no more. The swollen streams roared in the waterlogged combes, heavy rain was forecast, and people remembered an earlier occasion when, it is said, a grand piano was seen sailing down the valley with the survivors of a shipwrecked hen-coop clucking on its superstructure. Fortunately the heavy rain held off, although elsewhere in the West Country, at Kingsbridge in Devon and out on the Somerset Levels around Taunton, houses were flooded to a depth of several feet as rivers burst their banks and drowned the fields for miles around.

By the following weekend the temperature had climbed dizzily into the fifties. Celandines bloomed and skylarks sang over Eggardon, as if celebrating nature's astounding resilience. Spring, a ludicrous proposition only four days before, was on its way. But heaped under every westward-facing hedgerow, and running like a white scar below the western lip of the downs, relic drifts still lay ten feet deep in places, and the last snow did not melt until well into March.

22 February

The Somerset Levels

February fill-dyke certainly lived up to its name this year. Drenched by yet another vicious low-pressure system spiralling in from the Atlantic, the land could take no more. The entire West Country is saturated, with water trickling from every pore. It was cold again today, with early snow dying away and more rain setting in before dusk. Not too pleasant for an ordinary outing; but ever since Christmas I had been hoping to spend a day on the Somerset Levels, and the combination of cold and wet weather with its promise of floods and wintering wildfowl was too good to miss.

The Levels are no great distance from my home – less than 15 miles as the crow flies – but the change in the landscape is dramatic. I drove north through Beaminster, crossed into Somerset south of Crewkerne and headed on through Martock under the high promontory of Ham Hill, source of the mellow, honey-gold stone which embellishes so many fine parish churches and mullion-windowed houses in the surrounding villages. Already the lie of the land had altered significantly. Gone were the rounded hills and folds of the Bridport hinterland. Here the landscape is more open and undulating as it sinks towards the Levels. Once all these south Somerset pasturelands were walled about by hedgerow elms: a secret country of lost lanes and quiet villages whose names ring like Sunday bells: Tintinhull, Chilton Cantelo. Then, in the early 1970s, came the Dutch elm plague. For Somerset, where elms were as common as weeds, it was a disaster. One by one the trees sickened and died, leaving a ghastly vision of winter-in-summer while the leafless hulks still stood. Today the scars have healed and only a few old stumps remain, but the illusion of hidden countryside and the blowsy beauty of its great elms have gone for ever.

Beyond Martock the land changed again. The fields levelled. The horizon had become as flat as the Fens around Ely; and the road now ran on a raised causeway with a ditch on each side, embanked by willows. I took a left turn just past the village of Long Load, and the transformation was complete. Here were the moors of Muchelney: the flood meadows of the River Yeo.

'Moor' is a word which rests uncomfortably among these sunken Somerset fields, but that is what people call them in the land of the seven rivers. Axe, Brue, Cary, Isle, Tone, Parrett, Yeo: into these sluggish streams pours all the run-off from the surrounding hills. The result is more like East Anglia than the West Country: 150,000 acres of flat, spongy pasture stretching from Taunton to the Mendips, willow-bordered and waterlogged, criss-crossed by dykes, known here as rhynes. In places the moor lies nearly 20 feet below the high-tide mark in Bridgwater Bay. Records from the time of Charles I describe parts of it as being covered by the sea for months on end. And even now, every winter, in spite of modern pumping systems and intensive new drainage schemes, a few grassy reaches still revert to watery wilderness. It is the last great English fen.

Somerset Levels, looking towards Burrowbridge

Somerset withies

The roadside fields swarmed with lapwings. Crests erect, they were moving through the grass hunting for worms. With them were smaller flocks of golden plover, beautiful in their black and gold spangled plumage. They were part of a total invasion of some 200,000 'goldies' which regularly winter in Britain, seeking out old, unimproved pastures such as those of lowland Somerset, where they are often found in the company of lapwings. Sometimes, startled by the predatory shape of a passing hawk, an entire field of birds would take to the air in a frantic rush of wings, the wheedling cries of the lapwings underscored by the plaintive piping of the smaller, faster golden plovers, until the danger was past and the swirl of birds would subside once more, falling like a soft blanket across a more distant part of the fen.

In winter there is a constant movement of birds across the Levels: rook, starling, black-headed gull, fieldfare, redwing, wigeon, snipe and kestrel; but the abundance of plovers paints a misleading picture. Most of these birds were visitors, migrants from Scandinavia and central Europe which arrive here after their breeding season and remain through the winter, while our own breeding lapwings fly south to warmer haunts on the Continent. The fact is that both the green and the golden plover are declining as breeding species in many parts of Britain. Golden plovers – birds of the summer uplands – have seen their breeding haunts vanish under a rising tide of new forestry plantations; while the green plover, or lapwing, has fallen victim to the massive conversion from pasture to ploughland which has changed the face of England. In the past twenty years, many English counties have seen a fivefold reduction in the number of breeding lapwings. For the survivors, these winter feeding grounds between the green hills of Somerset are vital if their numbers are not to shrink further. Yet new drainage schemes and a drive for more efficient farming may conspire to change the face of the moors permanently. It is a nightmare that constantly haunts both the Nature Conservancy Council and the RSPB, who regard the Somerset Levels as one of Europe's most important habitats for wetland wildlife.

At Muchelney, some twenty years ago on a day such as this, I watched short-eared owls swooping on voles among the ruins of the tenth-century Benedictine abbey. Then, the low-lying fields still flooded in winter, and Muchelney – the 'Big Island' of the West Saxons – was regularly marooned. The rising waters had driven the voles on to the diminishing circle of higher ground, and the owls – wandering hunters from Scandinavia – grew fat on the unexpected feast. But today there were neither floods nor owls; for here, as elsewhere on the moor, the great winter inundations were a thing of the past.

I drove on through Curry Rivel, high and dry on the narrow spine of hillier ground that heaves clear of the fens between Langport and Taunton, then dropped down over Red Hill with the whole of West Sedgemoor spread out below: a flat green plain of pasture and withy beds, cross-hatched by the precise geometry of lodes and rhynes. Bundles of withies stood in the fields; others were stacked by the roadside, awaiting collection. Sedgemoor's wet acres were ideal for the osier trade, which sprang up here in the nineteenth century in response to the Victorian craze for wickerwork. Fewer withies are grown today, but the club-fisted pollards are still cropped each year to produce the supple wands which, boiled and stripped of their bark, are the raw material of the Somerset basket weavers.

By the time I reached Stathe the snow which had earlier settled lightly on the fields had almost vanished, but the day remained cold. Stathe is a typical Somerset fen village, huddled against the raised banks of the Parrett: a straggle of low thatch and pantiled roofs, neglected orchards festooned with mistletoe, and kitchen gardens smelling of cabbages. Yellow light shone from cottage windows; otherwise the place seemed deserted. The village pub, the sinister-sounding Black Smock, was closed; but later the eel catchers would come, with their broad Somerset accents and talk of the beer money to be made with a lamp and a dip net when the elvers were on the move.

The mass migration of the elvers is an annual phenomenon in the land of the seven rivers. Long before the first cuckoo, the baby eels reach the West Country in their millions, the last lap of an epic journey from their spawning grounds in the Sargasso Sea in the North Atlantic. Borne to Britain on the Gulf Stream current, they arrive under cover of darkness, a midnight army of transparent, wriggling bodies, match-stick thin, two inches long, seeking the ponds, streams and ditches where they will grow into adult eels. In Somerset their progress is aided by the fierce Bristol Channel tides which send a three-foot-high wall of water surging up the Parrett. When the tide recedes it is as if someone had removed a giant bathplug. The river runs out so strongly that the elvers are forced towards its banks; but they continue to swim upstream – 'crawling' in the local vernacular – and it is then that the fishermen can make a killing.

In the old days the elvers were mostly caught for local consumption. Fried in bacon fat with an egg or two to bind them together, they provided a tasty seasonal treat for the fenland families. But in recent years live elvers have become the subject of a lucrative export trade, raising prices to such a height that moonlighting netsmen can earn several hundred pounds in a season.

Lapwing and golden plover

There is no mistaking a night when the elvers are crawling. All down the Parrett, from the Black Smock at Stathe to the King Alfred at Burrowbridge, the will o' the wisp glimmer of lamps and torches reveals the presence of silent figures, large dip nets at the ready. It does not do to ask questions. The fishermen are as slippery as their catch, close-mouthed and wary of strangers since the Inland Revenue began to take an interest in their activities. Sometimes a hint of violence charges the air, for competition is fierce and some fishermen even arrive in mid-afternoon to stake out the best spots.

Downstream at Burrowbridge stands the Mump, one of those strange, enigmatic hills which dominate the Levels. A landmark for miles around, seen from afar it resembles a pyramid, its slopes terraced by the tread of sheep, its summit crowned by a ruined chapel dedicated – like so many hilltop towers – to St Michael. Now I climbed the Mump's steep flanks, at the top of which the ruins stood open to the sky. I could find no shelter from the searching wind but the view was incomparable. In every direction green fields stretched away, a land as level as the sea, crossed by long lines of willows, the grey gleam of dykes and rivers, the flash of water where rain and snowmelt lay on the grass in rows of of parallel depressions, revealing the site of ancient gripes, or field drains. Far off in the mist rose shadowy hills: the Quantocks, the Brendons, the Poldens, with Glastonbury Tor and the Mendips beyond. Looking down on Athelney, where the fugitive King Alfred hid from Guthrum's Danish warbands, it took no great effort of will to re-create the primeval Saxon fen which covered nineth-century Wessex with its fathomless reed jungles, booming bitterns and secret tracks through the swamps.

Like all marsh country, these Somerset lowlands are sparsely settled. Farms and villages are widely spaced, hugging the islands of higher ground; and in winter even the cattle are taken to drier pastures or covered yards, leaving the fields for the birds. The skies are immensely wide. The long lodes cut across the meadows, creating endless perspectives of stunted willows and pale reflections. Yet for all its sense of space and distance the world of the moors is curiously introspective; stark to some eyes, but also full of unexpected drama and beauty, a low-profile paradise where marsh violets and bog pimpernel, frogbit and bur-reed, and the splendid royal fern, *Osmunda regalis*, grow. In summer a mingling of marshy scents rises: silt and watermint, the pungency of sweet gale. In winter, wild duck hurtle overhead in wild parabolas; and sometimes an eerie chorus of phantom horns falls through the mist as Bewick's swans come beating down from the cold north to settle far out in the emptiness of the old floodplain, high-

Grey heron

necked and watchful, murmuring with anxious voices.

Lost in the ocean vastness of the Levels, distant landmarks draw the eye. Church towers beckon across the fields, and you steer a course for them as if they were ships' beacons, burrowing down narrow roads that seem to run on for ever. To the north stands the tower of Weston Zoyland church, overlooking the plain of Sedgemoor where, on 6 July 1685, James, Duke of Monmouth and his rebel army were defeated at dawn by the royalist forces of James II in the last battle to be fought on English soil. When it was over, five hundred captured rebels were shut up in the church, where some died of their wounds, and twenty-two others were taken outside and hanged on the spot.

From Burrowbridge I drove to Weston Zoyland and back in a great circle, stopping near Middlezoy to walk out into the meadows beside a flooded rhyne. Some of these old ditches were begun in the Middle Ages by the monks of Glastonbury and Muchelney abbeys. Most were dug as drainage channels, but in a part of the world where stone is scarce they also take the place of hedges. Maintained at an artificially high level, a brimming rhyne is not only a perfect barrier for wandering cattle but also a giant drinking trough.

In the past the traditional pattern of low-intensity dairy farming has had little need for fertilizers or pesticides. Napoleon was still alive when the Levels were last sown, and most of the pasture has remained

Withies stacked at the edge of West Sedgemoor, Somerset

unbroken by the plough. But if the water table were lowered the land could yield arable crops, and with the help of nitrogenous fertilizers lowland Somerset could become the granary of Wessex. But the effects of chemical run-off and the drying out of the land would be disastrous for wildlife. As for the cattle, there are now modern machines that can dig a quick, deep ditch, and spring-loaded 'pasture pumps' which the cows can operate themselves, so that a high water table is no longer important.

I passed a colonnade of willows, all recently pollarded, showing fresh orange wounds where branches had been amputated to encourage new growth. Where sallows had also rooted in the rhyne the buds were breaking to reveal fat, silver-grey catkins, as silky soft as rabbit's fur. Where the trees ended, the dyke ran on between brittle palisades of bulrush and phragmites. Snipe arrowed away into the murk with harsh, scraping cries. A heron flapped heavily towards the Poldens. Further off across the fields a buzzard sat hunched in a dead willow, and a fox-red kestrel put up a swarm of starlings that swung in the wind like smoke before returning to earth in a wide circle of dark, rushing wings. Wherever I looked there was life and movement. But I wondered: would my generation be the last to hear the music of the winter swans and know the magic of the moors when water shines from every field? I hoped not. . . .

After lunch I drove north over the Polden Hills and then out across the peatlands of Avalon between Glastonbury and the sea to meet Tony Holley, a solicitor by profession but a man obsessed by the mysteries of animal behaviour. For the past eight years he has lived under the shadow of Brent Knoll, a solitary outlying Mendip tump, studying the secret world of the brown hare. Surrounded by the ancient open pastures of the Levels, Tony's house is also his hide. There he has converted his loft into a comfortable watchtower from which he can observe his subjects with an American astronomical telescope so powerful that you can see the whiskers on a hare's nose at half a mile.

Hares have always been creatures of mystery and superstition. The old English poem called 'The Creature No One Dares to Name' gives seventy-two alternative ways of alluding to:

> The stubble-stag, the long lugs,
> The stook-deer, the frisky legs,
> The wild one, the skipper,
> The hug-the-ground, the lurker.

Even today, the life of the brown hare is obscured by widely held misconceptions; but months of patient and solitary study by Tony Holley – on average he spends at least a thousand hours a year glued to his telescope – have now dispelled two of the most popular myths: the legend of 'March madness' and the belief that rival males box each other to win the favours of a female.

One reason why March has always been associated with the crazy courtship rituals of hares is because the grass is still short at the end of winter, enabling an observer to see every movement in the fields. From April onwards, as the grass grows taller, the hares become harder to see. But in fact, says Holley, there is no significant difference in their breeding behaviour throughout the season, which begins in January and continues for the next eight or nine months. Hares, being mainly nocturnal, spend most of the day resting in their forms – shallow scrapes or depressions in the grass. Holley has discovered that, summer and winter, hares need to spend about fourteen hours a day out of their forms. In winter, when the days are short, most of this activity takes place unseen, in the dark. But in March, as the days lengthen towards springtime, for the first time in the year hares can be seen as they leave their forms towards dusk to indulge in the frantic bouts of chasing and fighting which hitherto have taken place during the hours of darkness. March is the only month in the year when the grass is short enough, and the days long enough, for this behaviour to be observed.

Hares have a high rate of reproduction. A jill may produce three or four litters a year, and will come into season and breed again within a week of giving birth. At such times she will attract a gathering of maybe half a dozen jacks, all eagerly waiting for the day when she may be receptive. But there is always a hierarchy of males, headed by a dominant jack who jealously guards his female and is constantly chasing away the subordinate males. 'Yet in all the time I have been watching hares,' declared Tony Holley, 'I have never seen a real fight between two males. All the boxing bouts I have ever witnessed involved a female and a male.' The reason is that the females are much larger than the males – common among birds but unusual in mammals. Thus, if a jack persists in his unwelcome attentions, the jill will turn and rise on her hind legs to fend him off with her forepaws. If he is still aroused he may then also rise up and box back to defend himself.

As a result of these love bouts the males become quite battle-scarred as they grow older, especially about the ears, and the marks help Holley to identify individual animals. Living within the 250 acres of his study area there are about six jacks and five jills, all of which he can recognize from his rooftop window. Most familiar is Bolingbroke, a veteran jack which he has watched since 1981. Apart from their bouts

OPPOSITE: *Female kestrel*

OVERLEAF: *Brown hare sketches, Somerset Levels*

Hares
Brent Knoll
— Somerset
5/April/84.

colours
before
first
light

early morning
lighting

grooming

of sexual activity, Holley's hares are fairly solitary creatures, with males and females living in overlapping home ranges of 150 acres or more. The beauty of watching them from his loft is that he is never seen. 'Sometimes they come so close when they are fighting that I can hear their short explosions of breath just across the lane. They don't pull their punches; and there are times when the fur really flies.'

In late February the hares of the Levels normally leave their forms at around 5 p.m., but today the first jack began to move around soon after 4.15. Oblivious to the flocks of redwing feeding all around him, he nibbled at the soaking grass for several minutes, then settled down and once more lay still. Through the big telescope I could see every detail in sharp focus: long, white whiskers, lustrous eye, the long ears with their black tips laid back across the shoulders, the thick winter coat with its hint of rust around chest and flanks. Hares have extraordinarily keen senses: lying in its form, a hare can see through an arc of 320 degrees and catch a footfall down the wind two fields away. They also have the ability to remain quite motionless for long periods. Martin Knowelden, the wildlife artist, once told me how to distinguish between a crouching hare and a stone. 'If you see it move,' he said, 'it's a stone.'

A fine drizzle began to drift in from Bridgwater Bay, obscuring the distant cloud-grey slopes of the Mendips. In the failing light, just before 5 p.m., another jack which had been guarding a nearby female moved away and began to feed; and further off, another. These old, unimproved pastures at the foot of Brent Knoll are ideal for hares, but elsewhere over much of Britain the brown hare is in trouble. Bad weather could be partly to blame, with a run of cold, wet springs spreading disease and inhibiting the females from becoming pregnant. And always there are the hungry foxes, for whom the leverets are a favourite food. Scientists at the Game Conservancy have found that in parts of Britain a typical breeding fox family might consume as many as sixty-nine hares in a year. But there seems no doubt that the main cause of the hare's decline is the drastic change in farming practice, which has resulted in bigger fields, reduced the diversity of crops available as food, and ploughed up much of the ancient pasturelands which are still the hare's favourite habitat.

The brown hare is a true creature of the open grasslands. Unlike the rabbit, born in a bolt hole, blind and naked, a hare can see from its very first day – it is born furred and active in the field. Here it must live, alone under the sky, relying on its senses, its uncanny alertness and astonishing speed. The hare is a natural survivor, but it will need more than sharp eyes, a fair turn of speed and a high reproduction rate now that intensive agriculture is tipping the balance against it.

25 February
Powerstock, Dorset

As often as not at this time of the year I wake to the sound of sheep in the fields across the valley. On cold mornings the bleating of lambs, the deep-throated *baa* of the ewes and the rheumy cough of the old rams carry far on the wind. Their cries are strangely reassuring: a timeless sound in these western hills, for sheep and Dorset are inseparable. For a thousand years the sheep has been Britain's most important domestic animal. In the Middle Ages, ours was a wool economy. The handsome, half-timbered towns of Suffolk and the soaring stone churches of the Cotswolds were all paid for by the golden fleece.

Now, as then, the shepherd's year starts in September when he prepares for the following year's crop of lambs. The ram is fitted with a harness smeared with raddle – a mixture of iron oxide powder, paint and grease – to mark the ewes he will cover. The lambs will be born some twenty-one weeks later, in February. Like all ancient professions, the shepherd's life has a language of its own, rich in archaic words. At market time there is talk of crones (old ewes) and cuckoo lambs (those born after mid-April), of gimmer lambs (unweaned females) and hoggs or hoggets (female or uncastrated male lambs between weaning and shearing). A good shepherd is not only the guardian of his flock but also a dog handler, shearer and dietician. Like Hardy's Gabriel Oak he must be both midwife and doctor as well, able to recognize the whole Pandora's box of hideous diseases and parasites which can afflict his sheep: foot-rot, pulpy kidney, grass staggers, louping ill, scab (caused by mites), black disease (caused by liver flukes), and a host of ticks, tapeworms, lice, keds and maggots.

There are nearly forty different breeds of sheep in Britain, ranging from the hardy Scottish Blackface of the northern hills to lowland breeds such as the broad-backed and meaty Suffolks. The oldest and closest to the domestic flocks of Iron Age Britain are the dark brown Soay sheep of St Kilda. Around Powerstock the native breed is the Dorset Horn, sturdy, pink-nosed and prized for its ability – shared only by the Poll Dorset – to lamb at any time of the year. The rams are magnificent, their horns curled tight as ammonites; and in winter, when the flocks are put into the kale, their thick fleece soon becomes stained with earth, giving them the colour of lions.

My friend Brian Rice is something of a rare breed himself: a professional artist who is also a sheep farmer. Born in Somerset, he

OPPOSITE: *Lambing time*

126

just
arrived!

pink in lamb
from skin showing
through -

went to London and became a successful painter, part of the fashionable Chelsea scene during the flower power years of the 1960s. But he always retained his love of the West Country and an ambition to live and farm there one day. He still paints, and twice a week he teaches art at Brighton; but today he lives in Dorset where, for the rest of the time, he is out with his sheepdog, Hardy, tending the flock he has built up over the past six years.

Brian is no big-time sheepman – his modest flock consists of fifty-two ewes. Some are Scotch half-breeds, sway-backed animals with white faces and erect ears; the rest are Suffolk cross mules with Roman noses and the sooty faces of true Suffolks. To me, a layman, one sheep looks much like another; but not to Brian. He knows each one by sight, especially the ewe called Friendly, which he hand-reared and which now follows him around like a dog.

In addition he has three rams: two Dorset Downs and a pure-bred Suffolk. At the beginning of October the ewes had been put to the rams. Now every one bore on her fleecy rump the incriminating stain of red or blue raddle. The ewes with red rumps were those which had been tupped in the first sixteen days. The blue-rumped ewes were those which had been covered later. This spread the time of lambing, and also gave Brian some indication of which ewes would be first to give birth.

The ewes always know when their time has come, and wander off to seek a sheltered spot away from the rest of the flock. The birth follows quickly – usually within half an hour of settling down. If there are twins, the second lamb will normally appear within five or ten minutes of the first. So far only three lambs had been born: a single black-faced lamb whose spotted coat would disappear once its white fleece began to grow; and, from a Scotch half-breed ewe, twins with coal black feet and grey spots at the base of their tails. As soon as they were born, Brian had taken them into a barn which he had prepared as a crèche for the nursing mothers. Inside, using hazel hurdles bought at last year's Dorchester Show, a score of pens had been made up, with straw bedding and a bucket of water in each one.

Outside the day was raw. One ewe, a Scotch Whiteface with a red raddled rump, had taken shelter in the bottom corner of the sloping field. The wind was in the north and the sky was yellow with the threat of snow, but no snow came. Hazel catkins swung in the hedge and a missel thrush sang defiantly in the leafless wood; but spring still seemed a long way off. The ewe lay panting, sides heaving, her back arching in labour. But when her lamb appeared there was no life in it. Brian was crestfallen. Every dead lamb seemed such a waste. It was something he would never get used to. He picked it up and placed it in front of the mother so that she could lick off the afterbirth. Eggardon sulked on the skyline, blue with cold.

Late in the afternoon another ewe went into labour. It was a difficult birth. When a lamb is born the front legs should emerge first; but we could see only one leg. The other was stuck somewhere beneath the body; however, by carefully inserting his fingers under the small black nose and pink tongue, Brian was able to free the trapped foreleg. When the next contraction came it took only the gentlest pull on both legs to ease out the lamb. It was a fine big one. Brian picked it up and set it in front of the mother, which at once began to lick the afterbirth. This is an important ritual, for not only does it dry the lamb's wet coat, preventing the loss of precious body heat, but it also seals the bond between mother and offspring – the biological process known as imprinting. Two or three minutes later the lamb was on its feet, wobbly and unsure but already strong enough to stand.

Before it grew dark, Brian would move the mother and her newborn lamb into the warmth and shelter of the barn, where they could bed down in the sweet-smelling straw. Only then, long after he and the dog had gone home, and the fields were silent again, would the foxes come out of the wood to feed on what was left of the afterbirth.

27 February
Minsmere, Suffolk

Locked in the bone-clenching chill of an East Anglian winter, Minsmere lay silent under a pewter sky. Out on the sea wall a wind like a broadsword cut straight through my five layers of clothing. There was little movement on the mere; even in fair weather its marshland denizens are furtive creatures. The gnomish bittern – the eel stabber, the reclusive heron of the reedbeds – is seldom more than a ghostly booming voice; likewise the creeping water rail, grunting and squealing like a stuck pig at dawn and dusk. Today any wildlife around was sensibly keeping a low profile. Rails and bitterns sulked in the reed canyons, and only the wild duck seemed immune to the cold, riding head to the wind in bobbing rafts on the open water.

For nearly forty years Minsmere has been the pride of British bird reserves. This was the place where the avocet returned to breed after an absence of more than a century, and where more than half of all our marsh harriers are born. Leased to the Royal Society for the Protection

Tufted duck

of Birds by a sympathetic landowner in 1948, the reserve was later purchased for £250,000 to preserve these and other rare species.

It was a daunting sum to raise, but no one quibbled at the cost, for in conservation terms Minsmere is beyond price. Within its 1500 acres is a range of habitats which few other reserves can match: a rich mosaic of meres and reedmarsh, dunes, heath and swarthy woods. Its strategic position on the Suffolk coast provides a safe landfall for regular migrants, as well as unexpected Continental vagrants such as spoonbill and purple heron, which bring scores of twitchers from all over Britain. But above all, at a time when wetlands everywhere are under threat, Minsmere's wild enclaves have become a permanent refuge for some of our rarest breeding residents. Together with Leighton Moss in Lancashire it holds nearly half our breeding bitterns, and is virtually the last British stronghold of the marsh harrier.

Yet Minsmere's sense of inviolate wilderness is an illusion. This is no pristine Suffolk fen, but a man-made marshland of quite recent origin. Until the Second World War there was arable land here. Only when it was deliberately flooded as a barrier against invasion by Hitler's Panzers did the reedbeds take root and the marshland birds return. Today the delicate balance of competing habitats is artificially maintained by sympathetic management, without which the reeds would soon choke the open meres. Perhaps the greatest triumph of conservation management at Minsmere is the broad lagoon known as the Scrape. The biggest of the open meres, it is actually a fake, a clever imitation bulldozed into free-form shape, scattered with artificial islets of fine shingle and then inundated with brackish water to provide a suitable haven for terns and avocets. The success of the Scrape can best be judged by the fact that Minsmere is now the avocet's most successful British breeding ground.

Each habitat holds its own secrets: bitterns and bearded tits in the 400-acre reedmarsh, sparrowhawks dashing down the woodland rides, little terns along the foreshore. In early spring and summer, marsh harriers beat over the mere on mothlike wings, the cream-headed males resplendent in their rich chocolate plumage; and at dusk the churring of nightjars carries across the sleeping heath. But winter brings its own rewards: Bewick's swans with buttercup bills, all the way from Arctic Russia; shore larks, great grey shrikes and geese. It is now, emptied of human visitors, that Minsmere reveals a wilder, darker, altogether more elemental side, far removed from its nightjar summers. Alone under the low grey skies, among the impenetrable reeds and the chainmail glitter of the mere, the centuries fall away and Minsmere returns to the Dark Ages: a fen fit for Grendel.

The day was too cold for snow. I sat in a hide, sipped hot soup and watched snipe probing the marsh, looking for soft spots where the frost had not reached. Outside, there was no sound but the venomous hiss of the wind in the reeds. Inland, above the surge of woods, forlorn in the midwinter light, grey geese were flying. There was no sign of the bitterns, nor of the otters which once shared their domain. But towards dusk, crunching home through the frost, I saw three dark shapes spiralling over the hunchbacked heath: two hen harriers mobbing a short-eared owl.

Once much of East Anglia was like this – just reeds and birds and empty coast; shingle scrunching underfoot and the scream of gulls on the North Sea wind. Now Minsmere is one of the last wild places where marshland birds can breed in safety. Yet even here, like a symbol of the unknown future waiting at Minsmere's gates, a concrete monolith frowns across the marsh: the uncompromising silhouette of Sizewell nuclear power station.

28 February
Blakeney, Norfolk

Shore lark

In Blakeney I awoke to see a flight of mallard beating to windward between the houses, and waves lapping at the wheels of cars parked on the quay. Overnight the tide had turned and the sea had come stealing in to reclaim the land it had been losing over the centuries. Saltings and sandbanks that had dried in yesterday's pale sunshine now lay beneath a waste of grey water, and only the sea walls and the distant dunes of Blakeney Point stood clear of the waves.

All along the north Norfolk coast the great estates with their pheasant coverts and hedgeless 40-acre fields slide into a vast no man's land of tidal flats and drowning marsh. At low water you can walk over endless realms of seablite and eel-grass, on gleaming reaches of wave-ribbed sands that were seabed only hours before. If you come with a spade and know where to look, there are cockles to be dug by the sackful. But the tide's return is just as swift, filling the maze of muddy creeks with an audible gurgle, and it does not do to tarry too long on the marsh.

Looking back from the shingle spits and marching sandhills which are the new frontiers of the sea, the original coast was clearly visible beyond the dun colours of the marsh; a groundswell of the old land rising, a sullen wash of wind-burnt holm oaks, the encrustations of pantiled rooftops marking the silted ports of Cley, Blakeney, Wells and Brancaster. Dutch-gabled Cley, once a wool port, has a fine eighteenth-century windmill and a pub called the Harnser – Norfolk dialect for heron. Blakeney has a church tower whose beacon light once guided shipping to the town's broad quay. Wells is a warren of narrow back lanes that bring you to the Buttlands, a spacious green surrounded by lime trees and Georgian houses. Brancaster was once a Roman garrison, the northernmost fort of the Saxon shore, though they might as well have tried to hold back the tide as to keep out the Scandinavian sea raiders whose settlements gave Norfolk most of its placenames.

Everywhere in Norfolk, flint is king. Even the most modern houses sport flinty façades. Mostly, whole pebbles are used; after rain they gleam from the cobbled walls like small, polished skulls. But sometimes, as with the cavernous Norfolk churches, the flints are knapped, so that the light glints darkly from their opaque crystal cores. The result is a bleak beauty in perfect keeping with this austere coast.

In its time this off-beat edge of eastern England has thrown up some remarkable characters – not only the hardy old marshmen and wild-fowlers, but individuals like 'Coke of Norfolk', nephew of the Earl of Leicester, who revolutionized English agriculture; and the Reverend Harold Davidson, the notorious rector of Stiffkey who was unfrocked in the thirties for associating with 'loose women' and was later killed by a lion at Skegness. Norfolk's most famous son, Lord Nelson, was born just a mile or two from the sea in the village of Burnham Thorpe and has many a local pub named after him. Some are simply called the Hero – as if there could be no other.

Common seal

There is magic here at all times of the year, but perhaps never more so than in May and June, with the skylarks rising and redshanks fluting over the greening marsh. On warm days, when the tide has receded over the horizon and the dunes are too hot for bare feet to endure, when the air seems to melt and run flickering over the marsh, creating strange mirages in which the climbing surf seems higher than the land – then is the time to explore the miles of glistening sands beyond Holkham Meals, the knee-deep lagoons and cockle strands where ringed plovers scurry among drifts of bleached shells. Yet even in summer this is two-sweater country. There are times when the wind blows so strongly that the heavy pub sign at the White Horse in Blakeney flies horizontally; but provided you come well lagged against the weather the rewards are immeasurable. At Cley and Brancaster and a score of other spots, paths run out through the reedmarsh, or along the tops of the grass-grown sea walls towards the distant mumble of the breakers, and an emptiness of sand and shingle where the only footprints are your own.

Back in Blakeney at high water, I booked a boat trip to Blakeney Point, a wild shingle spit owned by the National Trust, whose disused teahouse, painted battleship grey and built on a heroic scale, like a garden shed by Brunel, stands marooned in a desert of marram-grass. There are no regular inhabitants here – only terns and oystercatchers, and common seals who returned my gaze with dark and trusting eyes as their sleek, whiskered heads popped up almost under the bows of the boat. If East Anglia has a Land's End, then surely it is this lonely, seal-haunted promontory.

MARCH

1 March
Powerstock, Dorset

Every day since Christmas I have been putting out bread, bacon rind, odd lumps of fat and other household scraps for the birds. The reward has been a constant procession of tits and starlings, blackbirds, finches, a pair of nuthatches and an occasional plundering crow. Peanuts seem to be the most popular food – especially with greenfinches. In very hard weather greenfinches depend almost entirely on garden scraps, which is perhaps why they exhibit such surprisingly aggressive behaviour towards other birds when feeding.

The most acrobatic entertainers are the great tits and blue tits, and the less common marsh tits, all of which feed by hanging upside down underneath the container; but the most spectacular visitors are the nuthatches, which breed every year in one of the three hollow oaks at the bottom of the valley. They are shyer than the other birds, but hunger has made them bolder, and they make regular forays, grabbing whole nuts through the mesh and then flying back to the oaks before coming back for more.

Throughout the winter the garden also attracts chaffinches, bullfinches, wrens, robins, dunnocks and song thrushes. Earlier, too, I was delighted to see an over-wintering male blackcap. Most of these warblers are summer migrants, but in recent years a few have chosen to remain all year in the milder southwestern parts of Britain.

Another welcome visitor has been a male great spotted woodpecker. A beautiful black and white bird, he swings on the container flaunting the scarlet feathers under his tail as he hammers at the bag of nuts. He has come less often of late, and today for the first time this year I heard him drumming in the orchard – a sure sign that spring is on the way.

OPPOSITE: *Badger in primrose wood*

OVERLEAF: *First signs of spring – primrose, common violet, lesser celandine*

135

overlap
sometimes

violet leaf

Spring flowers
Powerstock — Dorset
March/30/84.

Sweet
Violet

Lesser
Celandine

Primrose

Garden birds: great tit and blue tits

For his staccato rattle – a rapid burst of eight or nine hollow taps at a time – is both a challenge to other males and an invitation to females as a new breeding season approaches.

4 March

Powerstock, Dorset

Brian's flock had now produced fourteen lambs, including three sets of twins. One of the twin lambs was very small, an endearing bundle of black wool on long, spindly legs. Brian was trying to foster it on the ewe whose own lamb we had watched being stillborn the previous week, but so far she had shown no interest. If she continued to reject it, he would have to rear the lamb by hand.

Meanwhile the earlier lambs had grown enormously. Now they were outside with their mothers on the home pasture, rushing about in the sunshine. The wind was still in the north, but the air felt mild wherever there was shelter. Blackbirds carolled in the hedgerows, and for the first time this year I heard the full breeding song of a cock chaffinch. It is strange how young lambs seem to love standing on the tops of the grass-grown anthills – just like the topi antelope of East Africa, which stand for hours on the termite mounds of the Maasai plains. Other lambs butted at their mothers' udders, tails frisking furiously as they fed. Hardy the sheepdog was fascinated. He is redundant at this time of the year, and can only sit and watch, or beg to be thrown a stick. Blackbird and song thrush, the high, quavering bleat of young lambs and the deep, belching voices of their mothers – how welcome were these sounds of returning spring.

After tea I went down to the vegetable garden to prepare a plot for early potatoes. The wind had died away with evening and smoke rose vertically from cottage chimneys. I sank the spade in the ground and levered up the first heavy clod. The earth was cold, but as I pulled at the tangles of chickweed and groundsel the mild air soon filled with midges – another indication that, here in the south at least, winter's grip was slackening.

Around the cottage our garden snowdrops were fading fast. Primroses now took pride of place, with a scattering of mauve and white crocuses and a few audacious primulas. Lovelier still for me were the lowly winter aconites, whose gold petals open to receive the sun's warmth but close in a tight, frostproof ball before dusk. The winter jasmine – magnificent these past few weeks – no longer trailed its yellow stars along the wall, but the flowering quince had put out its first orange-red blossoms, and the lemon yellow racemes of *Mahonia lomariifolia*, dangling like pendant earrings among the prickly leaves, had begun to fill the air with their sweet fragrance. Suddenly, winter seemed an age. I longed for sun, for apple blossom days and long, light evenings by the sea. But spring would have to wait. In two days' time I would be travelling north to Scotland, to the high kingdom of the golden eagle where winter is not so easily defeated.

10 March
Glen Affric, Highland

The road into Glen Affric climbs between steep hills of birch: the gateway to a secret country of loch and forest and great sad hills where eagles sail on an endless hunt for winter carrion. As the road toils on, the first pines appear, a dark host of bristling shapes clambering from the gorge below. These are not alien conifers planted by the Forestry Commission in neat rows for quick profits, but self-sown native Scots pines. Here in Glen Affric, and in the shadow of the Cairngorms at Rothiemurchus, and at Beinn Eighe on the west coast, and in the Black Wood of Rannoch, are the last remnants of the Great Wood of Caledon, the primeval northern pine forest.

The Great Wood once covered more than three million acres. Wolves and wild boar roamed its trackless deeps with elk, lynx and brown bear. For centuries the pines grew undisturbed. Far to the south the Romans came and went. The Saxons fought over their Dark Age kingdoms. And the pines outlasted them all.

Then came the Vikings, and the war on the Great Wood of Caledon began. In the west they fired the forests and felled the tall trees to carve dragon prows for their longships. Slowly at first, but with gathering momentum, the Great Wood shrank and its forest creatures were hunted down. The bears were gone by the tenth century; the elk lasted three centuries more. Clearance was given added impetus by the invading English, who saw Caledon as a lair for wolves and rebels alike. The last wolf in Inverness-shire was killed in 1743.

The final blow which brought the Great Wood to its knees was the failure of the 1745 Rebellion. Forced to pay homage in material terms to their Hanoverian overlords, the impoverished clan chiefs sold off their timber to English ironmasters. Entire glens were emptied and hillsides cleared; but the pines of Glen Affric proved too difficult to dislodge. So there they remain, sadly reduced in number but still dense enough to provide an illusion of primeval pine forest, complete with its natural denizens: capercaillie and crested tit, pine marten and wild cat. In places the pines spring from fissures in the very lip of the gorge, leaning out over the hissing cascades and deep, cidery pools far below. Some of the trees are very old: among them are undoubtedly a few gnarled patriarchs which were rooted here long before Culloden.

On the near side of the glen the pines have not been spared. They were cleared at the turn of the century, and in their place the Highland birch – always so swift to recolonize – has moved in. History, which was cruel to the pines, was kind to the birches. They grew tall when the Highlanders who would have felled them left the glen to fight for their country in the First World War and were themselves cut down in the fields of Flanders. But birch is short-lived compared to pine. Today the Glen Affric birchwoods are dying on their feet, a glorious mausoleum of rotting trunks and crumbling stumps.

On Loch Beneveian the first red-throated divers had arrived. There was no wind in the glen, and the loch was a polished mirror which perfectly reflected the sombre pines. Through binoculars I watched the male, his feathers still flecked with winter white, draw a thin silver line across the water as he swam towards the grey female. Soon the loch would echo to their cries, and later, when summer came, they would fly away to nest among the flags and lilies of the hill lochans.

On Loch Affric a rind of ice glazed the surface, though the day had not been cold. A pair of teal sprang from the lochside and rose high into the air before turning away down the glen. I watched them go, two hurtling specks outlined against the snowy crests and corries of Tom a'Chòinich.

It is now well over a decade since I first slogged up Tom a'Chòinich. That was the first time that I had smelled the incense of the pines and seen at close quarters the wildlife of the Scottish Highlands, the blue hares, golden eagles and wild red stags which haunt these bleak and unsparing summits, so remote from the world of men. Then, as now, my guide was the naturalist and author Sir John Lister-Kaye. As a young man he had thrown off his urban shackles to work on a wildlife book with Gavin Maxwell. When Maxwell died in 1969 he struck out on his own and set up his own business, taking visitors into the hills of Inverness-shire to watch wildlife in some of the most beautiful surroundings in Europe. The enterprise prospered and he moved on down the Beauly River into a rambling Victorian country house, complete with Gothic turrets and a hall filled with ancestral portraits, which he converted into a thriving field studies centre.

When the house was built, a century ago, people came to Scotland to shoot a stag or kill a salmon. Now most visitors are content to walk and observe; but they still need a guide to unlock its secrets, and this is the niche which Sir John Lister-Kaye has found. His vocation is new to the Highlands. He is a man who dresses like an old-time ghillie in tweeds and plus-fours, stout brogues and a battered deerstalker, but who carries binoculars instead of a gun. He knows the hills in all weathers, and every plant and wild creature from the moss underfoot to the eagle in the sky. One day he may take you to the Beauly Firth and walk you half a mile on your elbows to listen to the anguished chunterings of a thousand pink-footed geese feeding in a stubble field. Another day he may drag you off into the misty blur of a Highland dawn, through dripping birchwoods where lichens hang like peeling paper, to surprise roe deer in the meadows and maybe see an otter in the River Glass, and certainly, if it is winter, to watch wild whooper swans and hear their sad bugling, like a piper's lament, hollowing the early morning glens.

And one day, you may be sure, will be set aside for Tom a'Chòinich, the Hill of the Moss, home of the ptarmigan and white mountain hare. By alpine standards it is a mere hummock: 3600 feet of peat bog, rock and icy corries; but these gaunt Highland summits dominate the landscape out of all proportion to their size. *Beinn, meall, cairn, sgurr* – no wonder the Gaelic language has so many words to denote a mountain.

These are not hills in which to walk alone. It is beautiful country, but without mercy. Stay here too long, you feel, put one foot wrong or lose your way in a blizzard, and you would be sucked into those hungry hillsides like a dead stag. The silence is unnerving, the sense of melancholy overwhelming. Where does it come from, this aching Highland sadness that tugs so sharply at the heart? Is it the absence of all the people who once lived here before the Clearances and who now haunt the glens with their unseen presence? Are theirs the eyes that make you feel you are being watched from above and behind? Often when walking in the Highlands I have felt the hairs rise on the nape of my neck, and have turned round only to see an emptiness of hills, and maybe a deer on a distant skyline.

On my last visit we had walked along the summit ridge of Tom a'Chòinich with snow buntings drifting away from beneath our feet, and tremendous views spread out before us, to Mam Soul and the Five Sisters of Kintail, the cloud shadows racing, the light falling silver on lonely lochans marooned in a desolation of heather. But today we had no plans to explore the high tops. Instead we returned to Cannich and drove into Glen Guisachan, where John had lived ten years earlier.

Crested tit

We left the vehicle and walked into a wood where relic Scots pines still grew among dense new strands of spruce and larch. The oldest of the native pines are easy to identify with their spreading crowns and sturdy trunks. They are known as 'granny pines', and may be up to three hundred years old. 'When I first came to the Highlands there were still 53,000 acres of Caledonian pine in Scotland,' said John. 'Now two thirds of them have been felled.'

The wood was as quiet as a church. We followed a forestry path into its resinous gloom and almost at once put up a magnificent cock capercaillie. The bird must have been feeding on the fresh green pine shoots, but we did not see it until it flew off. It was the size of a turkey, yet in flight it was as silent as an owl. We had only a fleeting glimpse, and against the sky we found it impossible to make out the glossy green throat and startling red eyebrows; but at least I had seen the elusive caper – the giant grouse of the Caledonian pine forest.

Higher up the hill we emerged from the trees on a rise of moorland. Patches of rotting snow still lay in the hollows beyond the deer fence, and John described how, during one particularly severe winter in the 1970s, the deer had been driven off the hills by a terrible blizzard. They had come down in the night to seek shelter in the woods but could not get past the fence. Next morning their frozen bodies lay piled against the wire. And as if to underline the harshness of these winter hills, we came to a burn in which a pile of driftwood had become snagged where the water flowed under the fence. Staring out from the dead branches was a stag's antlered skull.

Moments later we heard a gruff bark, and froze. Less than forty paces away, a roe buck was watching us. Again he barked, and then came cautiously forward, sniffing the air. He was a superb specimen: his winter coat was thick and dark, with a prominent double collar of white fur beneath his throat, and his antlers, still in velvet, stood at least twice as high as his large, cocked ears. 'What a beauty,' whispered John. 'A silver trophy if ever I saw one.' I could not believe what my eyes were telling me, that the buck had not recognized us as humans, for he was still coming forward, sometimes stopping in mid-stride, one foreleg raised. Could he have mistaken us for a rival buck, trespassing on his territory? Then suddenly he had our scent and was away, hobby-horsing over the heather until he reached the skyline. There he paused to stare back at us, ears wide, head proudly erect; then he turned and was gone.

Capercaillie

12 March
Glen of the Eagles, Highland

The long glen led westward, and we drove into it along one of those single-track Highland roads, following a shallow river which sparkled over beds of bright pebbles. Glen of the Eagles is not its real name, but it would not do to be more specific so long as eyries continue to be robbed by egg collectors. Every year for as long as anyone can remember, a pair of golden eagles have bred in this awesome defile. They are one of about 400 pairs which make up the Scottish breeding population, which is now one of the largest and most important in Europe. The golden eagle is Britain's biggest native bird of prey. From bill to tail it can measure over three feet, and its wingspan exceeds the height of most tall men. In the air, long wings outstretched, it looks like a flying door.

Golden eagle

We parked near the river beside a sandy spit where I found otter tracks and a fresh spraint on a tuft of grass, and the scattered vertebrae of a sea trout like a broken necklace of white beads. There were alder trees along the bank, as old and as gnarled as a grove of Greek olives.

One side of the glen was raked by sunlight, but the other stayed in deep shadow. I scanned the high tops with binoculars and picked up a mantle of crows feeding on a rotting stag, but nothing more. Inch by inch we glassed the crags, looking for likely nesting sites or even a glimpse of the birds themselves. We found two old eyries but no sign of recent activity. Last year's nest – an untidy stick pile the size of an armchair – had been blown down from the crags by the great storm which had raged through the Highlands on 2 January. At Aigas, said Sir John Lister-Kaye, the wind had sounded like an express train hurtling over the roof.

Golden eagles are conservative birds. Not only do they mate for life but they remain true to their ancestral eyries. Some sites have been used by generations of eagles – yet most pairs have at least one alternative eyrie in their home range which they will occasionally decide to use. So it would be with this pair. If last year's nest had been destroyed, they would use one of their other favourite ledges. There, all through February, they would have brought a steady airlift of dead sticks and heather stems. Where pine is plentiful, an eyrie that is used regularly can grow to resemble a cartload of kindling several feet high. But this new nest would be smaller, and much harder to find.

We sat and waited. The sky turned dark and a sudden squall sent

snowflakes racing towards us across the heather – to be followed by brilliant sunshine which struck sharp, silver glints from the river and picked out the pale trunks of birches straggling up the glen's steep flanks. A thousand feet above us, snow was still falling in grey shawls around the topmost crags. Somewhere up there, we were sure, was the new eyrie.

Silence, as deep as a well; then we heard a sudden, gull-like yelp: *kee-yow*. And there was the bird which my friend Mike Tomkies, the Highland naturalist and author, calls 'nature's dark angel of death', sailing out from behind the ridge. Even at such a height there was no mistaking the awesome silhouette of that seven foot wingspan. Through my binoculars I could see the bunched talons that grip like a bench vice, the crooked slate and gold bill, the fierce, frowning eyes that glittered as the wedge-shaped and strangely reptilian head swivelled this way and that to scan the ground beneath. Then the eagle began to soar, lifting and turning in majestic circles until it was lost in the hanging cloud.

An hour passed, and a second eagle swung into view. This was the male, a smaller bird and easy to recognize because of a prominent gap in the trailing edge of one wing left by missing feathers. To see both birds was good news indeed. It confirmed what we had suspected: that this was a breeding pair with eggs in the nest, and we had just missed the changeover when the female had returned unseen to relieve her mate. Now she would be settling down for her turn at incubation, but we still could not find the nest. The male, meanwhile, had ringed up into the blue and then slid away over the hills to hunt for hares. An eagle's life is an endless treadmill of hours aloft, scouring the high tops for food. It has been estimated that to feed a typical eagle family for a year takes the equivalent of one dead stag, 110 hares and 160 ptarmigan.

By now the afternoon was almost gone, but still we waited, hoping to locate the elusive eyrie. A merlin appeared on the other side of the glen, sharp wings flickering as it dashed over the heather and disappeared behind a cliff. Immediately a pair of ravens shot out from the cliff, croaking loudly before rolling and diving back to the ledge where the female had been sitting since the end of February on four blue-green and brown-freckled eggs. In the Highland year ravens are invariably the first birds to nest.

At 4.15 the familiar, cloud-biting shape of a peregrine appeared in the western sky, hunting over snow-flecked hillsides which the setting sun now bathed in an unearthly yellow glow. Once the sun was down, the light faded fast. Dusk came flooding through the glen, bringing

144

stags out of the hills to browse among the birches quite close to the road. It was time to leave. We turned round for one last look at the crags – and there was the female, aloft again. Once more she had outwitted us and slipped from the nest without being observed. Up there, a blizzard was brewing. Now, huge wings held out like boards, she was flying in the teeth of the wind, oblivious to the skirls of snow which had already swallowed up the hills behind her. We should have to come back again if we wanted to find her eyrie.

13 March

Strathglass, Highland

We were going up the Grey Glen on dawn patrol to look for that most elusive of British mammals, the otter. John has a 200-acre farm here, called Carnoch, meaning the Field of the Rock. It is a marvellous place of wet, rushy meadows and alder groves with the River Glass running beside it. Some of the land is grazed in summer by beef cattle, but the rest is kept as a nature reserve: a home for heron, cormorant, goosander, teal and goldeneye. In winter there are whooper swans, and in summer sandpipers. At dusk the red deer come down from the hills. Roe deer creep from the surrounding birchwoods, and at night foxes, wild cats and pine martens hunt voles in the wet meadows. But best of all, John's two-mile stretch of riverbank is a breeding ground for otters.

Daylight was already seeping down the glen when we arrived, but a full moon still hung over the ghostly corries of Beinn a'Bha'ach Ard. We parked the Land Rover and walked out through the melting frost towards the winding river. In the bankside alders, a flock of siskins swung like wind-blown leaves among the cones. There were fox scats in the grass, thick with the fur of voles, but we were not looking for foxes. We walked on upstream, squelching over black rotting alder leaves. Out in the open a buzzard mewed as it rose from a post and flapped heavily towards the distant woods. Overnight flurries of snow had dusted the hills well down below the treeline. Now, in the windless dawn, soft flakes still fell, drifting like feathers; yet the valley echoed to the singing of thrushes. In spite of the snow, the air was soft this morning. Even so far north, winter was drawing to a close.

In its deeper courses the river was as black and polished as obsidian. The snowflakes melted as they touched its surface and vanished without trace. We continued, conscious that wary eyes were watching. No matter how careful we were, our presence sent ripples of alarm

OPPOSITE: *Female merlin*

OVERLEAF: *Otter, River Glass, Scottish Highlands*

surging through the valley. Teal jumped from rushy pools left by the river's former meanderings, and two whooper swans flew away upstream, bugling mournfully. To the Celts the whoopers were birds with music in their wings – a romantic description but one more suited to the goldeneye, whose flickering pinions truly whistle as they rush overhead. At a time when wildlife everywhere is in retreat it is heartening to see this dapper little duck establishing itself as a regular Highland breeding species. It first nested here in the early 1970s; now some 200 goldeneye chicks are hatched in Scotland every year.

After about half a mile we found fresh otter tracks clearly imprinted on a sandy scour below the bank. John reckoned they were only a few minutes old, so we followed them upstream, trying to conceal ourselves behind a row of alders. Beyond the trees, where the river widened, we found more evidence of recent activity: fresh spraints on the turf, and the remains of a salmon. In winter the otters feed on the spent kelts which have finished spawning and are drifting downriver to die. This fish must have been dragged ashore and eaten in the last few days. Now all that was left was the broad tail and sturdy backbone, and a curling lower jaw, or kype, which showed it to have been a cock fish.

Still crouched over the skeleton of the salmon, I heard John's excited whisper and looked up to see two otters staring at us from the far side of the river. They were swimming just under the bank: two fierce, whiskered heads raised inquisitively in our direction. One dived almost at once. The other remained for at least a minute, as if intrigued by our presence; then it, too, submerged.

Moments later it reappeared and ran up the bank, whistling loudly as if looking for its companion. In colour and texture it was as grey and slippery smooth as the water-worn alder roots amongst which it now sniffed and searched, snaking in and out of holes, running along a fallen trunk and galloping through the bankside grass. On land it romped along with a sinuous porpoise roll, displacing its thick fur so that it was no longer sleek and glistening but bristled with sharp points.

Back in the water again, it swam directly towards us, still piping anxiously and pushing a bow wave along with its blunt nose. We sat on the bank, scarcely daring to breathe. I could hardly believe my luck. It was extraordinary behaviour for a wild otter, and I could only assume that this was a youngster which had not yet learned to fear man. Only when it was within 20 yards of us did it turn and dive. Even then we were close enough to follow its course upstream by the bubbles which drifted up and broke in a long silver chain.

We followed its progress with binoculars as it swam unhurriedly round a bend in the river. There the first otter was waiting. Was this the mother of the youngster we had been watching? Then together they swam on, romping and splashing upstream until they entered the shade of a distant alder grove and we could watch them no more.

Red stag

All my life I had wanted to see a wild British otter. Now I had seen two in a morning. I looked at my watch. It was fifteen minutes since the otters had first appeared. Even John, who sees otters regularly, was thrilled. 'You know,' he said, 'this farm has given me more pleasure than anything else I have ever owned.'

15 March
Glen of the Eagles, Highland

We were off again to the glen, determined to find the eagles' nest. After arriving at mid-morning we had been watching for hardly more than five minutes when the male with the missing pinion sailed overhead. He drove directly towards the crags and settled on a ledge to the right of a deep gully which had spewed a fan of grey scree through the birches hundreds of feet below. Hurriedly I set up John's telescope and trained it on the hunched silhouette of the eagle, just in time to realize that I had found the eyrie – a massive pile of sticks and heather at the back of the ledge – and was about to witness a change of watch as the male shuffled forward to relieve his mate. Even as I watched, she rose from the nest and launched herself from the cliff to loft away over the glen. When she had gone, the male climbed into the nest, rearranged his wings and then very carefully settled down to cover the eggs. Once in place he was almost invisible except for the dark wedge of his tail, and it was easy to see why we had not found the eyrie before. In all respects it seemed an ideal site: well hidden, virtually inaccessible and clear of the snow which now plastered many of the surrounding crags and hillsides.

We stayed throughout the afternoon but did not see the female return. Indeed, apart from the pair of resident ravens who croaked and tumbled in the updraughts, the entire glen was unusually silent. In the marshy pools beside the track, toads had gathered to mate and spawn. In another month each peaty pool would be seething with tadpoles. It had been a typical Highland March day of fleeting sun and sudden snow showers; but in late afternoon the clouds dispersed to give a last hour of bright sunshine. As the low light streamed down the glen, the hillsides which had seemed so empty now came alive with stags. Every sweep of the binoculars picked up a fresh group – some lying quietly in

Pine marten

the heather, others silhouetted against the skyline, where they looked quite magnificent with their spreading antlers. At close quarters, however, I could see that many were thin and scrawny and in poor condition after the unsparing Highland winter. These were the survivors. The weak, the sick and the lame had long since perished. Some had died of pneumonia; others had sunk in black bogs, too enfeebled to haul themselves out, or had frozen on the open hills to become carrion for crows and eagles. Their deaths were cruel, but the scavengers saw to it that they had not died in vain. In winter, deer and other carcasses can provide the golden eagle with up to 40 per cent of its diet.

Later, as we were returning to Aigas in the dark, our headlights picked out a pair of gleaming eyes in the road. The apparition was the size of a small, thin cat, but had the typical rippling body of a weasel and a bushy, flowing tail. Held as if mesmerized by the beam, it rose on its hind legs, revealing a creamy bib that stood out boldly against the thick chocolate fur which covered the rest of its body; then, quick as a snake, it was gone. Such was my first and only glimpse of a wild pine marten, perhaps the rarest of all British mammals.

Like all members of the weasel tribe, the pine marten is congenitally inquisitive, quick and alert in its movements, and an agile climber.

Who can outclimb the squirrel
But the weasel of the trees?
Who can outrun the roe deer
And catch the hare with ease?

So ran the words of a nineteenth-century hunting song. But although the marten does eat squirrels, its favourite prey consists of mice and voles. It will also take eggs and incubating birds in spring, and feed on berries in autumn and spent salmon and other carrion in winter. When the kits are born in April they are no bigger than mice, and they remain in the den until the beginning of June. The den itself may be hidden among rocks, in a hollow tree, or sometimes even in an old eagle eyrie.

A thousand years ago the *taoghan*, as it was known in Gaelic, was quite common in Scotland. Records from the tenth century mention the sale of marten furs for 24 pence, and these pelts were greatly valued until well into the seventeenth century because they lacked the rank smell associated with other members of the *Mustelidae* family – hence the pine marten's old name: sweet-mart. But by the turn of the century the pine marten had disappeared from the Hebrides and was extremely rare on the mainland. Elsewhere in Britain a few pairs clung on in the more remote parts of Wales and the Lake District. It looked as if the pine marten was heading for extinction; but in the 1920s the tide began to turn in its favour. Today, helped by the spread of conifer plantations and a more tolerant attitude among many landowners, these elusive and fascinating creatures are beginning to expand southwards from their Highland strongholds.

25 March
Powerstock, Dorset

I came back from Scotland to find that spring had already begun to infiltrate the sheltered combes and vales of home. At last the grass was growing green again. South-facing hedgebanks were thick with primroses. In the moist shelter of Castle Lane the delicate flowers of moschatel had appeared, sprouting from the banks like miniature green clocktowers. Everything seemed so much more advanced down here in Britain's Deep South – we must be a month ahead of the Highlands. Already the glossy leaves of cuckoo pint were unfurling, together with green tongues of ramsons, whose garlic pungency fills the lanes when the white flowers bloom in May.

All winter long I had watched with mounting impatience as our garden became increasingly more sluttish and weed-infested; but even our well-drained hillside tilth had been too sodden to work. Now the gales seemed to have blown themselves out. The year was on the move again and we would have to dig fast to keep up with it. Last Wednesday had been the official first day of spring, but the weather had made it impossible to start on the garden until now. Potatoes were the first chore. It had been potatoes that set us on the road to partial self-sufficiency eight winters earlier. Now our gardening year had come full circle once more, with open eggboxes of seed potatoes spread out on the floor around my desk. Down here in the southwest it was already mild enough to plant our earlies – Arran Pilot – whose dark eyes had now sprouted healthy, greenish purple shoots. But our maincrop, 14 lb of Désirée, would have to wait another month. Of all potatoes, this is my favourite: pink and plump, deliciously rounded; perfect for roasting, delicious when baked in its jacket. No other vegetable was better named: Désirée, sweetest and sexiest of spuds! What's more, these heavy croppers have a reputation as good keepers. Dug up in September, they would see us through until the following spring.

Last night the clocks went back, giving us an extra hour of precious daylight after tea. This, for me, marks the moment when winter's grip

Pussy willow catkins

is truly broken, even though the woods are bare and the wind still blows with an iron ring. To celebrate the first light evening of the year we walked down the valley to West Milton and found a bank with wild daffodils in bloom where we had not·seen them before. Rooks cawed loudly in the tall trees. The birds had returned to the rookery a month ago; now they rose and fell above the treetops, or stole twigs from each other's nests. As we passed underneath, the din was deafening. They spewed from the spinney, their rasping voices pursuing us: the immemorial sound of early spring in an English village.

But still we had seen no chiffchaffs. By now the first of these pale, leaf-thin warblers should have arrived from their winter quarters in sub-Saharan Africa, slipping through the valley bottoms to gladden the ear with their own name, whispered again and again from stream-side alders. The spring migration was late this year.

OPPOSITE: *Powerstock, Dorset*

BELOW: *Rookery*

30 and 31 March
North Cornwall

The journey seemed shorter than I remembered it. As a child, going to Cornwall by train was a daylong adventure. Now you can board an Inter-City express at Paddington and be over the Tamar in four hours. But the familiar landmarks were still there beyond the carriage windows: the sedgy jungles beside the Kennet and Avon Canal, the Westbury White Horse marching across the Wiltshire downs, and, best of all, the widening estuary of the Exe at Torcross, herons hunched at the tide's edge and the sight of the sea almost beneath the wheels of the train as it purred down the coast under the Old Red Sandstone cliffs of Dawlish.

Even when very small I used to stand in the corridor so as not to miss that view, nose pressed against the window until long after the train had passed up the Teign estuary to Newton Abbot. Further west, at South Brent, slopes of dark bracken swept up and away to the rim of the great moor where sometimes you might glimpse wild ponies on the skyline. Then high over Brunel's rumbling bridge with its dizzy views of grey warships in the Tamar roadsteads, and one had the feeling of leaving England for another country, older and infinitely more mysterious, incised by damp valleys of mouldering oaks where the vanished locomotives of the Great Western Railway puffed through the sky on echoing viaducts.

So Cornwall became my first love, long before I lived in Dorset. Even then, the tug of the west had taken hold, which holds me to this day, the feeling of the sea taking over, the land running out as you follow the sun. Cornwall taught me that beauty in landscape, as with people, goes more than skin deep. It is bone structure that counts, and Cornwall has the lean, spare beauty of land long exposed to the elements. There is no fat on it. You can feel its ribs through the turf under your feet, and see where the quilted fields fall away to reveal a gaunt breastbone of granite running from Bodmin Moor to the treeless parishes of West Penwith.

From Cornwall I learned also how weather can change a landscape, what happens when a sudden sea mist comes rolling in over the hedgebanks, and why so many artists come to paint the pure Atlantic light. In its winds and silences I listened for the mysteries of its saints and holy wells, and the lonely, wheel-headed crosses which spoke of Cornwall's Dark Age kings. But that was long ago. Now, after I had crossed the Tamar in twilight, a fine rain began to fall. At Bodmin Road the station walls glittered black and wet in the lamplight. The night air was chill, but it held that indefinable smell, perhaps of the sea, not so far off, and the acid odours of the ancient moor by which I would know Cornwall with my eyes shut.

What had brought me back to Cornwall was a man with a lifelong passion for the peregrine. If ever there was a man possessed it is my friend Dick Treleaven. For him there is no finer sight in nature than this yellow-fisted killer with the Genghis Khan moustache and harsh, heckling cry. Since time immemorial this magnificent falcon has bred on the great fortress cliffs of the Atlantic coast, and every week, in fair weather and foul, Treleaven is out there with them. 'Peregrines are an obsession with me,' he says. 'I love to see them cleave the air with that immense sense of purpose. For me they are the embodiment of the wild places in which they live.'

I first met Dick Treleaven nine years ago. He had appeared on BBC TV in David Cobham's splendid wildlife documentary *In the Shadow of the Falcon*, and I had been sent down to write an article about him for the *Sunday Times*. He is an immensely likeable man, as Cornish as his name, well-read, generous and amusing, and we have remained friends ever since. In his time he has been an infantry commander, painter and falconer. Now a widower in his sixties, he has sold the family business in Launceston and retired to a small bungalow in the village of South Petherwin, where a constant stream of friends and fellow peregrine fanatics come to take him out to the cliffs for his weekly vigils.

His long association with the peregrine began, of all unlikely places,

Peregrine territory, North Cornwall

in Piccadilly just after the Second World War. He saw a painting of a falcon in a shop window and decided right then that he had to paint birds of prey. If he wanted to paint hawks he knew he would also have to keep them. So in 1951 he took up falconry, joining the close-knit and eccentric brotherhood that met regularly at Hallworthy, in what was then still good country for Montagu's harriers, to fly their hawks on Bodmin Moor. His first hawk was a goshawk called Crasher, who came from Holland. 'I used to walk around Bude with the bird on my fist,' he said. 'One day I overheard these two kids talking as I went past. "There he goes," said one to the other, "old Plus-Fours and his bloody sparrow."'

Crasher was followed by a succession of sparrowhawks, a lanner falcon from Benghazi, and Sammy Snatchit, another goshawk who escaped and was last seen perched on a railway signal in Basingstoke. But he has never had a peregrine. 'They owe allegiance to nobody,' he declares. 'I know the peregrine is the falconer's dream, but I could never own one. It is too noble a bird to be captive. It has to be free. It belongs high on a clifftop, and that is where I like to see it fly and hear it scream.'

Arms waving like a conductor at the last night of the Proms, eyes ablaze with a wild, predatory gleam, he described the first kill he ever saw. 'I was out on the cliffs one June, sitting on a rocky spur 150 yards from the eyrie. A flock of pigeons came up the coast. Suddenly the old falcon flew out from the cliff. The pigeons turned to escape and came over my head. I looked back, and out of the sun came the tiercel, dropping like a stone. He came out of his stoop just below the flock, bounded up into them and picked out a pigeon as clean as a whistle. As I stood up the feathers drifted down over me. It was an incredible baptism.' Yet even for someone as patient as Treleaven, such moments are rare. 'It's like fishing,' he says philosophically. 'There's a hell of a lot of waiting for the eternal tug that never comes.' But that did not stop us from setting out for the cliffs for yet another long watch.

The way to the coast led down a narrow lane between squat hedgebanks of Delabole slate set in herringbone patterns, from whose cracks the fleshy leaves of pennywort erupted like green blisters. Where the lane ended on the open cliffs the ferocity of the winter gales had stripped the bracken until only the wiry main stems remained; yet even here, among the most sheltered tussocks and in south-facing hollows out of the wind, early primroses told of returning spring.

The day was cheerless, but the coast was alive with birds. Herring gulls hung in the updraughts, crook-winged, wailing, rising and falling about the pillars and buttresses of yawning chasms. Somewhere a raven grunted beneath an overhang. Fulmars gabbled as they planed over the swell and boomeranged around the cove before landing on guano-spattered crags, and above the mumble of the sea came the fretful piping of oystercatchers and the deeper, menacing bark of a marauding black-backed gull.

The wind was raw and we cast around among the lichen-scabbed rocks and sweet-smelling gorse thickets for a place to shelter while we glassed the black cliff on the far side of the cove, looking for the resident pair of peregrines whose eyrie was hidden at the back of a grassy ledge halfway up the rock face. Even before we found them we could hear them screaming, and suddenly they were below us, both birds together, flickering in from the sea. The falcon disappeared behind the headland, but we watched the tiercel land on a cushion of thrift and begin to tug at something anchored firmly beneath his yellow feet. Grey feathers began to float away on the wind, and we realized that we had just missed a kill. Most likely it was the falcon which had killed, and had brought in the pigeon for her mate, who was now greedily tearing red hunks of meat from the plumed carcass.

During the winter the falcon is the dominant hunter, so Dick believes. It is she who makes most of the kills, virtually feeding the tiercel. In winter, too, the peregrines range further afield, wandering inland to hunt plovers but still returning to roost on the cliffs. In winter peregrines can also be seen hunting teal and waders over the Camel estuary, but Dick's theory is that these are mostly the eyasses, or immature birds. The territorial breeding pairs stay closer to the cliffs, and most pairs remain bonded all year. 'They'll sit side by side,' he said, 'fly around on a bright day, displaying over their territory from late February onwards. Mating begins during the first week of March and, as a rule, the first eggs are laid at the beginning of April.'

On another part of the cliff a pair of ravens had lodged their nest of sticks in a narrow rock chimney. Their breeding season had begun even before that of the peregrines. For weeks the female had been sitting on a clutch of freckled sea green eggs. Now, although there were newly hatched chicks in the nest, both parents spent more time aloft, tumbling and flying in perfect unison, wingtip to wingtip, feet dangling. Sometimes one bird would peel away in a long, looping dive, only to rejoin its mate moments later, their black pinions almost touching, like outstretched fingers.

It was now nearly noon, and time for lunch. I dug into my backpack and unwrapped a pasty while Dick poured coffee from a flask into plastic mugs which we cupped with both hands to thaw our frozen fingers. We were about to enjoy a second cup when there was a sudden

LEFT and ABOVE: *Peregrine falcons*

commotion and every daw and gull on the cliff was aloft, wheeling and crying. It did not take long to find the reason for the turmoil. Halfway down the cliff the two ravens had cornered a buzzard on a ledge near their nest. The buzzard was clearly unhappy, and mewed plaintively as it sought to defend itself; but the ravens were merciless. Their throats swelled, their hackles rose, and their guttural barks rang around the cove as they chased the buzzard from ledge to ledge. At times it seemed as if they were deliberately baiting their victim. While one raven shuffled forward, croaking loudly, its mate would sneak up behind and tweak the buzzard by the tail. Once they almost forced it into the sea; but at last it managed to gain height and flap ignominiously to safety, mobbed by gulls until finally it took refuge in a hedge. Meanwhile the ravens, having tired of their sport, were performing a victory roll over the cliffs. High overhead the bold buccaneers twirled and tumbled. Their jet black plumage shone with glossy green and purple glints as they rolled in a single shaft of sunlight; then they were rollicking over the headland and out of sight.

So intent were we on watching the ravens that we did not see the falcon return to her favourite hunting perch high up under the lip of the cliff. One minute there was nothing but bare rock; the next she was there, alert and upright, glaring out to sea. Her sudden appearance is typical of the peregrine. How swift it is, how mysterious its secret comings and goings; assured and complete, it belongs to a world more ancient than our own, moved by visions we can only guess at, living a freedom we can never know. Here is a bird which is a masterpiece of aerodynamic design, a million times more complex than Concorde. When it stoops, diving out of the sun towards its quarry, its speed can exceed 200 mph; and its lustrous, lemon-rimmed eyes are eight times sharper than a man's. Dick Treleaven reckons it could read the small print in the *Sunday Times* from a thousand feet.

By now the sun had broken through, although the wind was as cold as ever, and both the falcon and the tiercel were aloft. 'God, how I love those birds,' said Dick. 'Just a couple of specks in the sky, but they dominate the landscape.' At first they seemed to be hunting and stooping with leisurely ease, almost playing with the pigeons which scattered in panic at every pass. Dick has a theory which divides the peregrine's aerial patrols into high- and low-intensity hunting. In a low-intensity hunt the hawk is moved only by visual stimulus, as when a flock of pigeons flies past: the natural response of a predator in sight of prey. The peregrine may stoop, but does not put its heart into it. Very different is the high-intensity hunt: then hunger burns inside the hawk, and the quarry is pursued to the death.

Brimstone butterfly

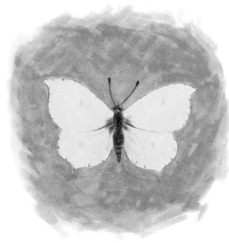

Pigeons are the prime target for Cornish peregrines. In winter they will hunt teal and curlew, fieldfare, lapwing and golden plover. They will also kill razorbills and they certainly take jackdaws to feed their young, although the adult birds seldom eat them, finding the flesh too rank. Once Dick Treleaven saw a peregrine snatch a pipit, and instead of flying to a rock to plume it she clutched the tiny corpse in her fist and ate it on the wing. We talked of the most efficient huntress Dick had known, a wild falcon he had nicknamed Kate. He had watched her and her mate, Idle Angus, for seven years, and once had seen her bring six pigeons to the eyrie in a single day. 'Now, alas, my beloved pigeon slayer has gone missing, and must be presumed dead. One day I must write a eulogy for her.'

The afternoon came. The wind dropped, and the sun became warmer. At the base of the cliffs a big, mottled seal bobbed like a bottle in the cove's green depths, then rolled and submerged to chase pollack through the kelp forests. Winter or summer, the magic of this savage coast never fails. On either side the cliffs fall sheer, sometimes breaking away to form barnacled reefs, dark islands and towers of bristling rock at whose feet the heaving swell booms and subsides with sinister gasps.

Ravens

Above us the falcon was back at her pitch. She has evolved a method of hunting which is ideally suited to the lie of the land and the predictable movements of her prey. When she leaves the cliff she flies like a fugitive, dropping swiftly towards the sea to disappear behind the headland. There she lets the upblast lift her, riding with it until she is once more in view. Inland, gulls are circling in a thermal and she glides towards them, ringing up on the warm currents of air until she is no more than a black star blinking among the crests and summits of the towering clouds. Now she drifts, going towards the sun, following the line of the coast for perhaps a mile, to the inlet where the pigeons breed. She has learned the ways of the pigeons, which leave the cliffs every day and pass up the shallow valley to feed in the fields.

From her lofty ambush among the clouds, nothing escapes her binocular vision: white specks of gulls glancing over the ploughland; black rooks and grapeshot bursts of starlings; but what she is looking for is the piebald flicker of feral pigeons. At once she accelerates. Her bow-bent wings beat faster, driving her forward with an unmistakable sense of purpose.

Unable to take our eyes off her in case we lose her, we cannot yet see what she can see, but know she is hunting. I remember Dick Treleaven's words: 'Peregrines don't really *chase* pigeons; their whole strategy is based on interception.' And it is true. Somewhere beneath her, as yet unaware of danger, a flock of pigeons are heading for home.

From a mile high the falcon tips up, folds her wings and stoops, faster than a falling stone. Her dive carries her below the skyline, where she is harder to see against the dun moor; but now for the first time we pick up her quarry. The pigeons scatter as she swoops beneath them and then flings up to snatch at a straggler. She misses – levels out over Hendra, skims on over bare fields, streaking low over the stone walls, slate-roofed farmsteads and squat church towers, the white gulls boiling in her wake – and misses again.

Now she rings up, turns and flies directly towards us. She passes overhead in an effortless glide, her wings dark blades, yellow feet bunched up behind. I can see her round head swivelling as she scans the ground beneath, and as she swings out over the cliffs the sun outlines her body in a wash of gold. Once more she climbs: the cloud biter, the beautiful barbarian, 'waiting on at her pitch' in the words of the old falconers, a thousand feet above the headland. Then another searing stoop, corkscrewing downwards to grab in play at a passing swallow. This time her dive takes her right into the cove, whipping low over the waves as if intent on committing suicide by smashing into the cliff; but at the last moment she bounds upwards almost vertically to alight on a buttress near the eyrie. Her triumphant scream floats back across the abyss.

My eyes were blurred with fatigue after squinting for so long through binoculars. I lay on my back above the crawling silver sea and felt for the first time the luxurious warmth of the sun's returning strength. For days the spring had been held back by contrary winds. Now the wind was in the west and spring was pouring over the West Country with the swallows. Somehow it seemed fitting that a winter I had begun by the sea, watching the departure of the summer migrants six months ago on Portland Bill, should end by the sea with their return. There was a softness in the air. Happily I closed my eyes and thought of home, and wondered how many swallows would nest in the village this year. By now a mist of green would be stirring in every Dorset combe and spinney. Even before I had left for Cornwall, the magpies' nests had been roofed with thorns, and a million celandines had starred the hedgebanks. Brimstone butterflies which had overwintered in the ivy walls of the Knap had already emerged to lay their eggs on the buckthorn's tender terminal shoots. Now, as the slow spring dusks grew longer, badgers would leave their setts above the orchard to snuffle along twilit paths soon to be buried under clouds of bluebells.

Swallow